# HORIZONS

## OF CHRISTIAN

### COMMUNITY

# HORIZONS

## OF CHRISTIAN

## COMMUNITY

*By Paul S. Minear*

THE BETHANY PRESS
ST. LOUIS, MO.

Minear, Paul Sevier, 1906–

   Horizons of Christian community.   St. Louis, Bethany Press
[1959]

   127 p. 20 cm. (Hoover lectures [1959])


   1. Church.    i. Title.

BV600.M53                        260                    59–10103 ‡

Library of Congress

To Anita

# FOREWORD

### The William Henry Hoover Lectureship
### on Christian Unity

THE DISCIPLES DIVINITY HOUSE OF
UNIVERSITY OF CHICAGO

The William Henry Hoover Lectureship on Christian Unity was established by the Disciples Divinity House at the University of Chicago in 1945. Resources for the lectureship are a trust fund established in the amount of $50,000 some years prior to his death by W. H. Hoover, of North Canton, Ohio. The purpose of the fund was designated as the promotion of Christian unity, a cause for which Mr. Hoover demonstrated a life-long interest. Originally the fund had been used for initiating publications, notably periodicals which have since become well established. With the successful launching of these enterprises it was decided that the cause of Christian unity could best be served by establishing at a major university center a lectureship on Christian unity since no such lectureship had yet come into existence. The Disciples Divinity House of the University of Chicago was asked to accept Mr. Hoover's trust for the purposes of sponsoring a lectureship on Christian unity.

The intention of those establishing the lectureship is that each lecturer shall be a distinguished Christian churchman of this or some other country, whose experience, research, and knowledge

7

eminently qualify him to discuss the problem of Christian unity and to make a positive contribution toward closer cooperation of the many Christian denominations and the ultimate unity of the church of Christ.

A series of lectures is normally to be given annually and to be published as the Hoover Lectures.

# PREFACE

The essays in this book represent an effort to appraise the scope of Christian community in terms of the thinking of the New Testament. They seek to measure the horizons of the life of the church—horizons which are ultimately the same for each congregation as for the universal company of those who bear the name of Christ. They seek to locate the existence of specific communities within these horizons, and thus to sketch the intangible diameters of the everyday life of God's people.

Such an effort is, of course, a symptom of contemporary concerns. For more than two decades in America men have been witnessing and sharing in a quiet (although noisily advertised) return to Christianity. This movement has been directed not alone toward a renewal of personal faith in Jesus Christ but also toward a rediscovery of the church as a unique form of human society. This rediscovery has, on the one hand, brought keener appreciations of fellowship within the congregation and, on the other hand, a more profound sense of solidarity with the Church Universal. The renewal has released strong impulses to formulate a doctrine of the church which would more adequately express both God's design for the church and man's experience within it.

These impulses have been felt by ordinary Christians on many Main Streets, felt first in a haunting sense that conventional ideas of what the church is have proved all too trivial and narrow to fit the reality. The pictures of the church carried in our minds are obviously out of date. They have been painted in an earlier day, often by those who have not glimpsed the glory now seen.

They have been set in a frame too small, a frame no larger than private experience in particular parishes. Our images of the church have been determined too much by our puny minds and provincial prejudices, not enough by the wide-horizoned story of God's people. Accordingly we look for more adequate images, not so much that we may be deceived by their greater glamor as that we may be rightly instructed by their overarching validity.

These impulses find their way not only into the work of theologians but also into the work of historians, particularly of biblical historians. Nor is this strange. Virtually every Christian communion recognizes the Bible as an authoritative standard for faith and action. To be sure, this recognition may be formal rather than real, official rather than actual. Even when a communion takes seriously its avowed norm, it often cautiously limits the range of concerns to which it applies this norm. For example, when a particular practice such as baptism is challenged, a communion may appeal immediately to passages in the New Testament which appear to justify its practice. But this communion may not listen so intently to the same New Testament to discover new light on what the real church actually *is*. Whether our sacramental practice is biblical is ultimately less decisive than whether our understanding of the church is biblical. Do we have an image of the church which is recognizably the same as that which is found in the New Testament? That is the more difficult and the more humbling question. Before we will be in a position to answer it, we need to pose a prior query: What comprehensive picture of Christian society does the New Testament itself provide? That is the question with which these essays are concerned.

Readers are urged, however, to remember two things. First, the purpose in what follows is not to present a formal, systematic doctrine of the church but to suggest the range and magnitude of the church's life. Second, the essays are addressed not to biblical or theological scholars chiefly but to thoughtful Christians who are interested in the theme and who have as resources their own used copy of the New Testament and their own memories of prayer and praise in a Christian congregation. These resources should help to clarify many ideas which would otherwise remain obscure.

The first four chapters, in substance, were delivered at the University of Chicago. The last chapter contains sections from the Dudleian Lecture at Harvard Divinity School. The essays have also been used in addresses at Meredith College and at the Howard University School of Religion. My cordial thanks go to friends who, on all these occasions, listened with surprising patience and who, by their sage criticism, prompted the revision of the manuscript. A special word of appreciation is due to Professors Raymond Morris, Joseph Sittler, and Claude Welch.

# CONTENTS

I. THE FULLNESS OF GOD'S GLORY      15

II. THE FRONTIER OF GOD'S WARFARE      39

III. THE CITY WHERE GOD DWELLS      59

IV. THE TIME OF THE CHURCH'S LIFE      81

V. THE SCOPE OF CHRIST'S WORK      103

13

# Chapter I

# THE FULLNESS
# OF GOD'S GLORY

This glory is preached and offered to us year by year, and day by day, and it is so great that no man, whoever he may be, can meditate enough on it, much less tell it in his own words. . . .[1]

—MARTIN LUTHER

[1]From *Day by Day We Magnify Thee*, Philadelphia: Muhlenberg Press, p. 7.

In one of his plays, Thornton Wilder elicits quiet laughter by employing various ways of locating "Our Town."[2] In the introduction to the play, this hamlet is identified as:

> Grover's Corners, New Hampshire,—just across the Massachusetts line: longitude 42 degrees 40 minutes; latitude 70 degrees 37 minutes.

Later in the play a geologist from the state university gives a more scientific description:

> Grover's Corners lies on the old Archaeozoic granite of the Appalachian range. . . . A shelf of Devonian basalt crosses it with vestiges of Mesozoic shale, and some sandstone outcroppings; but that's all more recent: two hundred, three hundred million years old.

When a minister from another town has occasion to write Jane Crofut, he addresses the letter:

> The Crofut Farm; Grover's Corners; Sutton County; New Hampshire; United States of America; Continent of North America; Western Hemisphere; the Earth; the Solar System; the Universe; the Mind of God.

[2]From *Our Town*, New York: Coward-McCann, Inc. © 1938. Used by permission.

It is thus relatively easy to locate almost any town on the map. Difficulties begin to emerge when we include environments which are not purely geographical. This is clearly the case with the Christian Church. From what meridian or equator are its longitude and latitude computed? What geographical formations constitute its ground? Where lie the horizons within which its existence is properly described? Like Grover's Corners, churches can rightly be located only by reference to an environment outside and beyond themselves. But this environment is a matter of much more than space and time. Its scope can be calculated only by measurements appropriate to the distances between the "Mind of God" and Main Street.

Think, for example, of your own congregation as it gathers on Sunday morning for its characteristic service of praise and thanksgiving. It will probably join in what is called the Gloria: "Glory be to the Father and to the Son and to the Holy Ghost, as it was in the beginning, is now and ever shall be, world without end." It will, as part of its credo, proclaim in unison: "I believe in the holy catholic church, the communion of saints. . . ." It will respond, more or less alertly, to a call to worship: "Behold, the dwelling of God is with men. He will dwell with them, and they shall be his people, and God himself will be with them." It will sit quietly as the pastor interprets some passage of Scripture, such as: "You have not chosen me, but I have chosen you." It will participate periodically in the sacrament of the Lord's Supper: "This is the new covenant in my blood." It will not leave the sanctuary until it receives a benediction: "The grace of the Lord Jesus Christ be with you." If other liturgical rubrics are used, they will reflect similar understandings and undertakings. To the degree that such activities are characteristic of your church, they become clues—essential marks—of what the church is. They serve to define the being and work of the church. They are snapshots of the church in action, moving images of a living community—not the only images, to be sure, yet mirrors which reflect in some degree the distinctive contour of a strange country.

Should someone suddenly confront a churchman with the question: "What makes a church the church?" it is likely that he would try to answer without mentioning such activities. The creed, the prayer, the sacrament—none of these may occur to him as essential to an answer. To him, the process of verbal definition may turn in quite a different direction. Often the definitions with which he is familiar quite ignore the activities in which he has been participating wholeheartedly. In fact, the need for definition may never have occurred to him. Year after year he has shared in the life of the church without ever posing or answering this particular question. He takes the church for granted. He knows what it is as a matter of course. So do the other members. The work of the congregation proceeds smoothly on the assumption that everyone knows what it means to be a congregation.

Once the question finds voice, however, it is not easy either to evade or to answer. If it is raised within a single congregation, for example, as part of a church school lesson, evasion may still be possible, for then the question is more or less a routine matter and members may fall back on some accepted formula which stifles rather than stimulates further study. But if the question is raised by someone outside the congregation, by a sceptical outsider, let us say, then the formulas which are common coin within the church may cease to meet the need. But if the question is raised in an interdenominational setting, where conflict arises among various Christian answers, then the easy evasions and the glib formal answers become painfully inadequate. In such a setting churchmen are often forced to confess—at least to themselves—that they are quite tongue-tied, unable to find the words which will communicate their deeper intuitions concerning the character of the church. And as the conversations proceed, the awareness of illiteracy grows steadily. Thrown on the defensive, some churchmen in embarrassment withdraw hastily from the fray. But not a few are unwilling to forfeit the game. Their interest in the church and their devotion to it are too strong. Inarticulate they may be, and even illiterate. But they are too honest with themselves and too engrossed with the question to make a shamefaced retreat, so they continue to study the question, in vigorous interchange with churchmen from other communions whose conceptions of the nature of the church are radically different from their own.

In this interchange two trends usually emerge. One is the tendency for perplexities to increase as all parties discover how far their own relatively simple formulas fall short of describing the whole life of the whole church. A second is the tendency for these perplexities to come to a focus around the problem of describing the interplay of God's activity with man's activity in the community's ongoing life. No view of the church long satisfies Christians themselves if it omits the essential work of either God or man. That is to say, the church is people, but it is a people called to a particular task by God. It is *the* people of *God*. And this fact requires a definition which will be both theological and sociological. In short, the true scale of the church's life includes the presence of both God and men. The congregation in Grover's Corners exists as a witness to the distance and the nearness of two realities: "the mind of God" and "Main Street." The root of many perplexities lies just here: we must speak simultaneously of the churches and the Church. We must be utterly realistic about the churches we know and at the same time faithful to the truth of the one holy, catholic, and apostolic Church. We encounter stubborn contradictions here, both in living and in thinking. We may try to ease the contradiction by a glib cliché about the visible and the invisible Church. We may fall back upon the obvious contrast between actual churches and the ideal Church. Should we turn toward theological definitions, we are haunted by the empirical state of particular churches. Should we try to describe these particular and peculiar institutions by sociological definitions, then our theological conscience begins to hurt. The more honest and intimate our acquaintance with both the church in Grover's Corners and the Una Sancta, the more difficult it becomes for us to conjure up a description which adequately copes with both. We carry in the same mind a sociological image and a theological image, and the two together produce a blurred vision. How, then, can we gain a comprehension of the church which will do sober justice both to the daily behavior of our own local fellowship and to "the noble company of the apostles"? Our view of the church should reveal the links between the smallest congregation and the communion of saints. It should locate the church in Grover's Corners both on the map of New Hampshire and on the map of heaven.

But this ability to relate the two maps is not noticeably present, at least not in most interdenominational conferences. When two Christians are gathered together discussing the church, the mind of one will be informed by a sociological formula, while that of another will be guided by a theological phrase. A third person may infer that the two are discussing two distinct realities, neither of which is the church to which he himself belongs. And rare is the group with a person who can detect beneath the clashing perspectives the common measure of truth in all, or who can discover a description of the church which articulates a genuine consensus. Even such a person will seldom find words which will fully reconcile the sociological stereotype and the theological stereotype.

This does not mean that contemporary discussions in this area are inherently polemic in tone. The sense of need and the mood of searching are rapidly displacing the angular petulance which accompanied earlier debates over irreconcilable positions. We are neither so self-confident nor so defensive. None of us can be so sure of his own conception that he can angrily repudiate all others. To be sure, the sin of stubborn pride is never far distant, but it is more frequently qualified by quiet reflection. If we join a group of Christians discussing this matter, it is not long before we notice that X has a hopelessly superficial notion of what the church is. Yet it may take but a moment of reflection to remind us that our own ideas were equally juvenile a very short while ago. "Thank God, *we* have discovered the church at a deeper level than he!" But this Pharisaic thanksgiving may be countered immediately by the thought: "a few years hence *we* will no doubt have moved to a level of comprehension from which our present stance will seem shallow." Thus we become more tentative and teachable in our present wisdom about the church. However impressive that wisdom may seem, to ourselves or to others, it continues to stand under the scrutiny of a yet higher wisdom. For many of us, there has been a time when our ignorance about the church was far greater than our awareness of the ignorance. Then there comes a time when our consciousness of ignorance begins to equal and then to exceed our ignorance. Current discussions concerning the church are qualified by at least a mild degree of humility because participants are reminded so often of the judgment which the Lord of the Church exerts over the Church, and of the judgment which the Church itself exerts over its amateur ecclesiologists.

Whenever we desire seriously to stand under this judgment and to learn from it, then we are on the way toward a new and more vital reading of the Bible. This is why the biblical conceptions of the church increasingly move toward the center of study and discussion, especially whenever ecumenical encounter brings into intimate conflict churchmen with radically different doctrines of the church. However passionately we may defend our own church view, we are usually aware that our thinking is all too thin when judged by the truth of the Church as it is in Christ. From him alone can we receive insight into the true scope of the Church's life. And for that insight we turn inevitably, although not exclusively, to the Bible.

The New Testament, however, does not readily provide neat solutions to our dilemmas. Those who expect from it authoritative pronouncements concerning the constitution of the Christian society are bound to be disappointed. This disappointment springs in part from the dearth of conscious efforts to define the church or to outline its charter and bylaws. It springs in part from the great profusion of images and pictures of the church, all of which are suggestive but none of which is put forward with authoritative clarity and finality. Judging by the variety and fluidity of descriptions of Christian community in the New Testament, we must conclude that the writers were much more flexible, imaginative, and versatile in their thought about the church than are we. The realities of communal life were more central to their thought, but the desires for systematic, explicit descriptions of that life were virtually absent. If we look for normative definitions, we will not find them; but if we look for intriguing insights into the distinctive texture of communal relations, we will be bewildered by the multiplicity of such insights.

## MYSTERY

We may illustrate one such insight, and the bewilderment it evokes, by observing that to several New Testament writers the realm of Christian community impinges at almost every point upon the realm of mystery, the *mysterion* of God. Initially, of course, the term mystery was used to describe not the character of the church so much as the unfathomable dimensions of God's wisdom, a wisdom which has been hidden from generation after generation and which no one can find by self-propelled search. No man can know God's mind or can offer him counsel, for he is the source and ground and goal of all things. (Romans 11:34-36.) The realm of mystery embraces as well the origin and power and fate of iniquity, of lawlessness, of demonic rulers. (Revelations 17:5-7.) It alone can comprehend the destiny of the races, whether Jew or Gentile. (Romans 11:25-32.) God's purposes and his actions spring from the abysmal depths of his wisdom and power. It would, however, be quite wrong to divorce the life of the church from the realm of this mystery, for otherwise, we would fail to comprehend a basic element in the emergence of the church.

Jesus' disciples were those to whom it was given "to know the secrets of the kingdom of heaven." (Matthew 13:11.) Apostles were those who had been made stewards of this mystery. (1 Corinthians 4:1.) The gospel which they proclaimed was a means of revealing this hidden divine secret. This gospel was quite futile apart from the power by which God exalted the crucified Jesus to a heavenly throne, an event, hidden in mystery, which the apostle was commissioned to announce. (1 Corinthians chapter 15.) It was inevitable, therefore, that, since the life of the church was inseparable from the life of the risen Lord, this life should be pervaded by the same *mysterion*.

In two writings, Colossians and Ephesians, this interpenetration of *life* and *mystery* is underscored. The operation of this mystery, in fact, can be said to constitute the church as the body of Christ. (Colossians 1:24-28.) It owes its very life to the truth that Christ indwells it. Implicit in this mystery is the truth that the sufferings of Christ, shared by the apostle himself, produce within the church as Christ's body both the wealth of glory and knowledge of this wealth. Because Christ himself is the mystery, the man who is made perfect in him shares in his treasury of wisdom and understanding. (Colossians 2:1-3.) Even more directly and fully is this doctrine developed in Ephesians, whose author traces to the same mystery the origin and power of such essential realities as grace and gospel, promise and power, boldness and faith. (Ephesians 3:1-12.) In brief, the relationship of Christ and the church constitutes a great mystery. (Ephesians 5:32.)

Wherever this mystery is present, men can see it or hear it only if the Holy Spirit enables them to see and hear. It is a secret revealed through faith and love and it remains a mystery even when thus revealed, because its status as mystery is due not so much to the ways in which we think about reality as to the very structure of reality itself. This means that the element of hiddenness derives first of all from the fact that we are in touch with a realm where the Most High God is active, where his will is powerfully at work, where the purpose which has been hidden for ages is being revealed. To say, then, that the church participates in this mystery is to say not only that its true substance, its essential being, is *not* amenable to the ordinary powers of sight and hearing, but also that this reality draws its life from the powerful presence of God.

This aspect of the church as *mystery*, therefore, links what has been said by way of introduction to what will be said in the ensuing chapters. If there is a renaissance of interest in doctrines of the church, this renaissance stems in part from the growing awareness of the mystery of the church's nature. If we are baffled by the complexity of this subject, this complexity is traceable to the same origin. If there are apparent contradictions between the "empirical churches" and the "Una Sancta," it is the status of the church as mystery which, at least in part, produces this contradiction and which alone can resolve it. If those who try to trace the boundaries of the Christian society are made humble by their task, it is the holiness of the mystery which in part evokes their contrition. It is the heavenly dimension of the church which fascinates us, nettles us, gets us entangled in the primary paradoxes of faith, and humbles us. But this very transformation of our approach may prepare us for fuller comprehension of the New Testament attitudes.

Such a comprehension is the very burden of one of the prayers in the Epistle to the Ephesians, a petition for Gentiles who have entered into "the stewardship of God's grace." They have received "insight into the mystery of Christ." This mystery suggests how and why as Gentiles they have been made "members of the same body as the Jews." They have been grasped by "the eternal purpose," have been strengthened by God's "Spirit in the inner man," have become "rooted and grounded in love." Christ has made their hearts his dwelling place. . . . All this has proved the power of the gospel of Christ. Even so, however, they stand in constant need of "power to comprehend with all the saints what is the breadth and length and height and depth." (Ephesians 3:18.)

The breadth *of what?* The depth *of what?* This is a question which is not answered. Is it the height of the love of Christ? Perhaps. The breadth of the family of God? Perhaps. The depth of our fellowship "with the saints"? Perhaps. All these answers might fit the context. But another phrase provides a legitimate summary of all these dimensions: that you may have "power to comprehend with all the saints what is the breadth and length and height and depth" . . . *of the church*.

To comprehend the magnitude of the church requires divine power and wisdom, because the church's existence is visible token of the mystery of redemption. Since this mystery is spoken of several times in terms of the glory of God, it is perhaps safe to suppose that the dimensions of Christian community are derived from the dimensions of God's glory. This community's horizons may ultimately be as far-flung as the range of divine glory. Let us then explore the basic meanings of this word.

## The Glory of God

This exploration immediately poses several obstacles, for few words cover such a motley of meanings, meanings trivial as well as profound. In ordinary discourse it seems to cause no trouble. The daily paper speaks of new fame or distinctions being awarded to a ballplayer, a pugilist, a pianist, or a scientist. Glory is virtually identical with reputation. It indicates that a person or an institution has ample ground for pride and for boasting. In whatever profession, it marks a successful climb to the pinnacle of achievement. In whatever field of competition, it represents stellar performance by a team, a school, a nation. All men, it is assumed, seek for renown, whether by one road or another. Glory therefore becomes indispensable in describing the different degrees of success which attends the winners.

In common parlance, therefore, glory is something meted out to its heroes and leaders by society, a term used as often to prod individuals to greater effort as to crown those who have fulfilled the specifications. The word thus is stock in trade for journalists and public-relations specialists. It takes on peculiar connotations from its rhetorical uses. It thus becomes a prettifying word, a word evoking the sentiments rather than the reason. It belongs to the vocabulary of the politician or the popular poet rather than to the mind of the metaphysician or the sociologist. Its function is to adorn opinions of value rather than to define the substratum of reality. It belongs to the amenities of discourse, not to the verities of being. Its major status in grammatical terms is that of an adverb or adjective.

Yet this very secular word also does service in various religious contexts. In religious art it can denote the halo used to symbolize the presence of a saint. Or it can apply to the dignity of an ecclesiastical office or institution. Or it can refer to the splendor of heavenly reality and even to the effulgence of the divine being. Even in religious uses, however, it often imports a cargo of associations which are secular in origins. The glory attributed to God differs only in degree, not in kind, from the glory attributed to engineers or generals. The sentimental mood predominates. The rhetorical flavor remains. If the preacher dwells on the honor which belongs to God, his sermon is heard by ears long conditioned by the demands of "public relations." It is inevitable then that the term "glory" should suffer a subtle but significant prostitution in meaning.

Considering this basic prostitution of the term, the reader of the English Bible must be alert for mistranslation whenever the term "glory" is used for the Greek term *doxa*. (Special warning is needed in passages where the Greek noun has been rendered by the English adjective glorious, e.g., Ephesians 1:6, 18.) For whereas in modern idiom, few things are more evanescent than glory, in the Bible nothing is more eternal. Whereas in modern idiom few things are less substantial, in the Bible there is usually a stubborn, tough ontological claim. In our ordinary speech we seldom use glory as itself an active and potent reality. We therefore fail to catch the full realism of biblical writers when they speak of God's glory.

It is even more certain that we mistake the full intent of the New Testament witness to the church as sharing in the fullness of God's glory as, for example, in Ephesians 1. For when we speak of the church's glory, we usually assume that we are voicing a sentimental human reaction to a social institution, a reaction which immediately elicits what can be said in criticism of that same institution. Glory is a comparative term with us, used to distinguish the greater or less renown of various historical figures or institutions. When, for example, we laud the glory of old alma mater, we would be embarrassed if anyone should conclude that we were speaking with ontological seriousness.

In dealing, therefore, with this dimension of the church's life, it may be wise to use a more technical term which has not been so corrupted by human standards of fame and reputation. To indicate the distinctive coloration of biblical thought, we shall speak of doxology and of the doxological. *Doxa* is the Greek word for "glory." Doxology thus refers to the doctrine of God's glory. Often, of course, there are disadvantages in choosing technical terms in that they sound foreign and awkward. But in this case the awkwardness is in part dispelled by the fact that almost every Christian congregation regularly employs a doxology in its liturgy. Audibly and visibly it sings or chants: "Praise God from whom all blessings flow. . . ." However difficult the tune, it joins in the *Gloria Patri*. It is accustomed to prayers which conclude with the doxology: "To him be glory forever and ever." It adds its *Amens* to proclamations and prayers, central to which is the ascription of all honor and majesty to the triune God. Moreover, these acts of worship are not simply occasional and incidental vocal genuflexions, quite dispensable and meaningless repetitions. Rightly considered they are declarations of what constitutes this company of worshipers as the Church. They point toward the center and rationale of its existence. They are not isolated acts which are performed, but events in which the whole Church participates. Something happens here. The Church receives as well as gives. The doxology is a two-way channel of communication. It is a canal which carries commerce in both directions. The doxology is, in fact much more than *a doctrine* of God's glory; it is the living recognition, the living enactment, and the living reception of God's glory. The Christian congregation, therefore, may well consult its own experience as the Church for a sense of the reality of the doxological fact. Yet it will turn to the Bible for light on the wider implications of that fact.

Let us then review some of the elementary convictions concerning the doxological realm which loom large in the Bible. Here it is assumed that God's glory can alone serve as the origin and measure of true glory. *Doxa* is basically a noun, a substantive. It denotes God's very being: his life, his power, his activity, his fullness, his grace. God's life is his glory; his glory is his livingness. To see him is to see his glory. To see his glory is to come in contact with his power. Wherever God is active, there his glory is at work. And wherever he is at work, and men see his work as really his, there they behold his glory. Each theophany, in other words, is a doxophany, i.e., a manifestation of God's presence.

## DOXOPHANY AND DOXOLOGY

Stephen and John looked into heaven and beheld the *glory of God.* (Acts 7:55; Revelation 15:8.) In both cases this vision placed on their faithfulness the stamp of the sovereign power of God, to whom alone belong "salvation and glory and power." (Revelation 19:1.) This salvation, the object of "our blessed hope," is elsewhere described as "the appearing of the glory of our great God and Savior, Jesus Christ." (Titus 2:13.) This glory is associated with the unutterably brilliant light which surrounds God's presence (Revelation 21:13) and with the utterly incorruptible life which pertains to God's realm. (1 Corinthians 15:43.) *Gloria dei* is the life of God triumphant over death. To experience his power to raise the dead is to behold his glory. (John 11:40.)

Because everything God does is a doxophany, the heavens and the earth are full of his glory. As the Lord of glory, whatever he does is intended to manifest that glory. Doxophany is intended to produce doxology. Creation acknowledges the Creator's glory by its doxology. Singing this doxology, by word and deed, becomes the shape of the church's response.

The double movement embodied in this response is superbly illustrated by the vision to John the prophet in Revelation, chapters 4 and 5. One movement is doxophanic—the manifestation to the prophet of heavenly realities. Shown by the Spirit an open door into heaven, John saw a throne surrounded by twenty-four elders in white garments seated on twenty-four thrones and by four living creatures. Day and night without pause the twenty-four and the four sang:

> "Worthy art thou, our Lord and God,
> to receive glory and honor and power."

Then into this scene came the Lamb, the slain Lamb, who alone was able to open the seven seals of the scroll of life. At his approach to God's throne a new song burst forth: "Worthy art thou. . . ." In this song all creatures in heaven and on earth and under the earth joined. "To him who sits upon the throne and to the Lamb be blessing and honor and glory and might forever and ever!" Everyone fell down in worship.

The countermovement is doxological—the visible and vocal worship of God by the churches of Asia on the Lord's day. (1:10.) The praise of the elders and angels in heaven correspond to the actualities of congregational singing on earth. Here in Pergamum and Thyatira men were glorifying both God and the Lamb. Their prayers and songs penetrated the boundary between heaven and earth, joining in the universal adoration of God. The distance between the throne of God and the bent knees of the Christian conventicle was radically telescoped. The slain Lamb was even then walking triumphantly in their midst. God pushed back the horizons of heaven to include them; simultaneously the horizons of earth were lifted to include all that was happening in heaven. Thus the double movement—doxophanic and doxological—formed a circle large enough to include Creator and creatures within a single universe of glory.

Yet this universe, by its very nature, excluded another realm under the control of man's foe Satan. Satan's kingdom is built on an opposite principle, a principle which requires the repudiation of God's glory and the blinding of men to the true character of that glory. This reverse law is the law of self-glorification. The world becomes a province of Satan's dominion by exchanging *gloria dei* for "images resembling mortal man." (Romans 1:18-23.) Obsessed with *gloria mundi*, men fall far short of realizing their intended destiny. (Romans 3:23.) The only doxophany which can deliver them from slavery is that which comes in the fullness of the times to manifest the fullness of God's glory. In the face of Jesus Christ men may now behold God's glory in its fullness. Here is the final and perfect doxophany: "He who has seen me has seen the Father." (John 14:9.) Here also is the final and perfect doxology: "I glorified thee on earth, having accomplished the work which thou gavest me to do." (John 17:4.) The incarnate Word becomes the place where men may see and know the power of *gloria dei* in its conflict with *gloria mundi* and its triumph over Satan. This doxophanic and doxological work is most fully revealed when Jesus completed his ministry on the cross. Here he received a body of glory. He ascended the throne of glory, he banished death and Hades. He came in the glory of his Father with the holy angels. He turned the kingdom over to God who shall be all in all. At every point of the story, the way of Jesus Christ is the way of glory: God glorifying his new creation, the new creation united in glorifying God. Yet at every step, this creation runs into direct conflict with Satan's kingdom, drunk as it is with self-glorification. With every step Jesus paces out the boundary between these two realms.

It is this boundary which becomes decisive for the church, for the other boundary—that imaginary line between heaven and earth—has been obliterated. Wherever Jesus Christ continues to do his Father's work, there he succeeds in bringing many sons to glory. (Hebrews 2:10.) Doxophany is a way of describing his outgoing mission that has no limits in space or time. The other sons who enter this family immediately participate in this doxophany. Beholding in Jesus Christ the glory of God, they are drawn within the one kingdom of glory and become its ambassadors in the world. They are themselves "being transformed from one degree of glory to another." (2 Corinthians, chapter 4.) Their lives become "enacted doxologies" as they learn to "do everything for the glory of God," thus overcoming the world which lives by the opposite rule.

It is clear, therefore, that glory is a term which is essential to the biblical message, and a distinctive mark of Christian community according to the New Testament. It is equally clear that modern Americans are accustomed neither to use the term nor to consider it a central component of the church's life. The idiom would be easier to grasp were we ancient Orientals accustomed to the image of kingship. For, in the ancient mythology, the true king could rule as the vice-gerent of God only if he had received the divine glory. His throne must be an earthly counterpart of the throne of God. The king does not seize power, but receives it as a gift from God. The gift indicates the king's total allegiance to God, which is the prerequisite for wielding his derived sovereignty. The delegation of authority to the king presupposes the king's acceptance of full homage to God. His robe, his beard, his throne and mace—these are symbols of this relationship.

The king, in turn, delegates or gives his glory to his retinue of servants, his ambassadors and courtiers. They share in the functions of his sovereignty, but only on terms of full allegiance to him. To accept from him a robe of honor means to accept him as lord and to serve him in the shared exercise of his sovereignty. Thus the royal glory is shared by the king with all of his servants and subjects, since all are bound together by one loyalty, one sovereignty, and one chain of responsibility. To break the chain, either by claiming independent "glory" or by rejecting the delegated task, is treason. And from the lowest link to the highest, the whole chain represents a gift of sovereignty from God, and an oath of abiding fealty to him.[2]

---

[2]cf. F. W. Buckler, *The Epiphany of the Cross.* Cambridge, 1938. My attention was called to this book by Professor Joseph Sittler.

If we lived in a culture permeated by such attitudes, we would no doubt find many biblical ideas easier to grasp. Even the Old Testament is nearer to that ancient outlook than the New. When the apostles looked for analogies to "the glory of God in the face of Christ Jesus," they found them in the Law and the Prophets rather than in political dynasties. One such analogy was provided by the figure of Moses. In 2 Corinthians, chapter 3, for example, Paul compares these two leaders of Israel. In the face of both Moses and Jesus the glory of God appeared among men. Through both, this glory signalized the sealing of a covenant with God's people. Through both, God was providing "ministers" for his covenant folk. In both cases God's glory was manifested in mortal bodies, in earthen vessels, without thereby ceasing to be transcendent power, belonging only to God.

Yet the glory conveyed through Christ excels at many points. It inaugurates a dispensation of life which does not fade away. It conveys the boldest of hopes because it lifts the veil between human eyes and the Lord. It conveys the abiding Spirit, and with this Spirit freedom. It transforms the community into the likeness of the Lord, from one degree of glory to another. The manifestation of this glory in affliction, persecution, for-sakenness, and death is nothing less than the manifestation of the life of Jesus in our mortal flesh. As this grace extends to more and more people, it leads to the antiphonal fullness of the doxology. This doxology binds Jesus to Moses, binds the church to Israel, binds every believer into the church, and at the same time enables all—Moses, Israel, the believer, the church—to share the final freedom and the final fellowship of God's eternity. Only a vocabulary which seems fantastic to ordinary human language can approximate adequate treatment of this tran-scendent historical phenomenon—the glory of God.

## GLORY IN THE CHURCH

We have now explored only a few of the ways in which the glory of God determined the horizons of community life according to the New Testament. We have been forced to ignore many of the implications of this particular horizon, but brief mention may be made of some of these. Consider the *moral* implications. "Everyone who exalts himself will be humbled, and he who humbles himself will be exalted." In the Gospels this law is illustrated by such everyday duties as the seating of people at table, and the waiters and waitresses at that table. Consider the *psychological* implications. Glory is manifested in the healing of the mentally sick. It is embodied in that self-emptying, self-forgetting, self-denying humility which turns despair into hope, and aloneness into fellowship. Consider the *sociological* implications. If the church is to be distinguished from other institutions, here is a fruitful place to begin. Where is there another social institution which knows in its heart that self-worship is the form of ultimate treason? Consider the *liturgical* implications. The deacon shall be the servant. Baptism is an enactment of becoming united with the dying-rising Redeemer. The Eucharist is a proclamation of the glory both hidden and revealed in his death. Hymns are public confessions that glory belongs to God and not to ourselves. Liturgy is the people's work of casting their crowns before the throne, of wearing the towel of service, of washing one another's feet. The corporate vocation is one of doing everything to the glory of God—in affairs of business (lord-slave), of family (husband-wife), of politics (emperor-subject).

Finally, consider the implications for the unity of the church. If there be only one faith, one baptism, one hope, it is because there is only one glory. If there is only one name, in which salvation operates, it is the name of one in whom all the doxophanies of God and the doxologies of men are perfectly and finally embodied. He it is in whom all the fullness of God's glory dwells bodily. He it is through whom God's glory becomes the fullness *(pleroma)* of the church's life. For the church to live as the body of Christ means that it embodies *his glory*.

It should by now be entirely obvious that no description of the church which omits this central aspect of its life would be true to the New Testament understanding. Do we think of the church as a family of sons of God? The New Testament identifies sons as those who inherit God's glory. Do we speak of a communion of saints? To the first Christians glory is the substance of sainthood. God glorifies the saints and is glorified in them. Do we prefer to think of the church as the people of God? To Saint Paul the people of God are those who have received God's glory. (Romans 9:4.) To Luke the coming of Christ was the sign that God had begun to fulfill his promise of "glory to thy people Israel." (Luke 2:9.) When the babe was born, the heavenly army sang the doxology and shepherds returned to their flock (there is church-symbolism here) glorifying God. (2:14, 20.) In a baffling phrase Paul speaks of Titus and certain fellow workers as "apostles of the churches, the glory of Christ." (2 Corinthians 8:23.) We stand amazed at this assertion. Does he consider these men, some of whose names are unknown, as Christ's very glory? Or is it the churches which constitute Christ's glory? In either case, the church is directly indicated as a doxophany of Christ, as Christ is the doxophany of God.

In his prayer in the Fourth Gospel Jesus speaks of the Church as those whom the Father had given to him, "Thine they were and thou gavest them to me." (17:6.) "All mine are thine and thine are mine, and I am glorified in them" (vs. 10). . . . "The glory which thou hast given me I have given to them, that they may be one even as we are one" (vs. 22). This oneness in glory is equivalent to oneness in knowledge of the truth (vs. 8), in the name (vs. 11), and in God's love (vs. 26). These are corollary and almost equivalent ways of describing the life of Christ in the church as the life of the church in God's glory.

No, we will never understand the church apart from understanding this glory. But on the other hand, the character of this glory defies academic definition, and therefore leaves us farther than ever from a satisfactory doctrine of the church. We can never reduce to order this profusion of texts, the kaleidoscope of contexts, the exuberance of imagination, the multiplicity of implications and nuances. The pursuit of precision is frustrated by the infinite flexibility of the Christian vocabulary. Glory is a word which plays havoc with any prosaic mentality. It breaks through all the pigeonholes of our mental filing cabinet: ethics, psychology, liturgy, politics, history, sociology, metaphysics.

It resists human use as a category of discrimination. It therefore does not often invade theological debates, simply because we cannot claim it as a tool for partisan polemic. If there is any one category of speech which places under immediate and ruthless scrutiny our best doctrines of the church and our best practices within the church, it is this: the church is the body of glory wherein the fullness of God delights to dwell.

The church is the fullness of God's glory. Yes, but this glory is the final and total condemnation of self-glory, of that glory which coheres in the drive-to-power of all human institutions. If we say that the church is sinless, we must measure this sinlessness by the total absence of self-glorification. If we are impressed with the sinfulness of the church, we must be aware that the glory of God appeared in the guise of sin and death. If we define the church as *eschatological event,* the *now* in which the congregation, through its response to Word and sacrament, inherits the promise, we must not forget that this glory is the same as that which encompasses the wide world's wondrous story. If we visualize the church as continuous with the apostles, with Israel, with Abraham and Noah and Adam, the links in this chain must be seen as doxological rather than as biological, sociological, or institutional. To use the category glory as a basic constituent of the church's life will not help us get an exclusive answer to ecclesiological questions, but it may help us formulate those questions. It may help us transcend the usual lines of debate. And in this very process it may open our eyes to the height and depth of the unity which we have in Christ, all the while it will impel us toward closer fellowship in the eternal doxophany and doxology.

Finally, let me suggest that the circle of doxophany-doxology which defines the scope of the church's life is the exact opposite of many vicious circles. It is noteworthy that although we have in usual conversation many occasions for remarking "What a vicious circle," we have not taken the trouble to coin an opposite expression. Is this a measure of our unconscious despair? Sin *is* a vicious circle. So is death. Every effort to idolize our own ecclesiastical tradition is a vicious circle. So too is every effort at shortcut schemes of Christian unity. But there is an opposing circle—a circle of grace, a circle of glory—where the enactment of forgiveness produces forgiveness, and where each doxophany produces doxology, where God glorifies his people—and his people cast all their crowns before him. Unless we remember that the Christian community is located near the center of *this* circle, and has as its horizon the whole range of God's redemptive power, then all our efforts to comprehend its unity and its mission will do little more than demonstrate the vicious circles of *gloria mundi*.

Chapter II

# THE FRONTIER

# OF

# GOD'S WARFARE

So long as this world lasts and the Christian Church within it, it is a militant Church, yet it has the promise that the gates of hell shall not prevail against it. But woe, woe to the Christian Church if it would triumph in this world, for then it is not the Church that triumphs, but the world has triumphed.[1]

—SØREN KIERKEGAARD

[1]From *Training in Christianity*. New Jersey: Princeton University Press, 1944, p. 218. Used by permission.

The Christian community, as we have seen, lives in constant contact with both heaven and earth, and therefore its horizons must include both. Whether we speak of its origins or of its destiny, its enduring ground or its recurrent worship, the Christian community has this double orientation. And any story which is oriented from and toward heaven involves us immediately in mythology. In this chapter, therefore, let us think first about the character of Christian mythology.

## Christian Mythology

Mythology is one way, and I think an essential way, of apprehending the hidden heights and depths of human existence. It is a way of relating the ordinary routines of daily experience to the cosmic and universal dimensions of reality. It assumes that the significance of events, while being inseparable from the events, yet transcends them. This transcendent significance stems from the truth that God is everywhere active in the activity of men.

In this sense, the presence of mythology may be detected in the simple straightforward narrative of Luke, chapter 10. Ac-

41

cording to this account, Jesus as Lord appointed 70 harvesters and sent them into the harvest field. Going as lambs among wolves they carried the healing message "The kingdom of God has come near to you." Some men were hospitable, others barred the doors. To one city the kingdom came with its peace, to another with a curse—a curse which portended a rain of fire and brimstone worse than that which obliterated Sodom. The response of cities to the visitation is described as bringing either an exaltation to heaven or a descent to Hades. When the disciples gave their report, they were so elated by their power to heal that they exclaimed: "Even the demons are subject to us in your name." In reply, Jesus gave an explanation of the source of their power: "I saw Satan fall like lightning from heaven." The disciples rejoiced because of their earthly power; Jesus urged them to rejoice because their names "are written in heaven." Throughout the narrative, scenes and events are described in terms of the decisions and actions of men and women, but none of these events bears its meaning on its more obvious surface. Each scene both conceals and reveals its connections with a much larger frame of reference. The Lord of the harvest is gathering his grain, but this fact is far from self-evident. The disciples are blessed because what they are seeing is, in fact, what prophets and kings had long awaited. Yet what *this* actually *is* remains quite hidden from the participants themselves.

We cannot pause long with this passage, even though its ambiguities invite closer scrutiny. But even this brief glance may suggest that the writer and readers of this story shared certain attitudes which enabled them to grasp meanings which elude us. Like other anecdotes about Jesus and his disciples, this narrative presupposes the presence among men of the living, active Lord of heaven. It presupposes as well the presence of the enemy whose fall from heaven is the signal for the spreading of conflict. It presupposes the nearness of the kingdom, expressed in the reality and finality of earthly healing and hurting. The story brings into immediate juxtaposition those heights of exaltation and those depths of humiliation which are assumed to accompany the response to a mysterious message. At every stage the narrator assumes a correspondence between earthly and heavenly events, a correspondence which filters only partially through Jesus' enigmatic words. The same double-image is mirrored by the disciples' journey, their equipment, their salutations and farewells, their ability to see and to heal. Jesus had been given power to comprehend the height and depth of what was happening. He sought to give his missionaries in turn a related and dependent power to comprehend the same height and the same depth. The truth he tried to convey was far more significant than the visible phenomena would in themselves betray.

Why, we must ask, do we find it so difficult to adopt this way of viewing reality? Surely it is because our eyes have been trained to perceive and to describe historical events in a very different fashion. What we often call a common-sense view of things is in large part a perspective and an idiom which we have learned so naturally that we are quite unready to grant the validity of alternate perspectives and idioms. Let me try to outline the hidden axioms of our own world view. This is hazardous, of course, because extreme diversities and wide variations exist. No one picture will suffice. Yet for clarity of thought an extreme caricature may be justified, if the caricature calls attention to lines which are really there, but which, because of familiarity, have lost their sharpness.

The sharpest, basic contrast is perhaps this: whereas in the biblical perspective God is everywhere alive and fearfully active, in our modern perspective God is dead, no longer at work creating and sustaining and judging. His life no longer serves as the touchstone of what is alive and what is real. Anthropology has replaced theology as the queen of the sciences. Man is himself consciously and voluntarily the center and determiner of history. In fact, man is man only insofar as he makes himself or becomes himself in and through historical decision. He wills to affirm his own autonomy, and he does this by limiting "the zone of absolute reality" to the manifest operations of men. Necessarily, then, he views history as composed of events and acts which transpire exclusively on the human level. These events carry their own value in themselves. Events move forward irreversibly and without regulation or control, but are themselves autonomous. The succession of events lies wholly within a time sequence, a temporal process, which is ruled by the laws of irreversibility and endless succession. This process cannot be abrogated, nor terminated, nor transcended. Any change in pace or direction is inconceivable. Ceaseless change and endless duration loom up as final barriers to any direct personal relationship to eternal reality. In fact, the existence of the eternal is implicitly excluded. Everything except inexorable time or the fixed laws of man's historical existence is relative. As Dilthey phrased it: "The relativity of all human concepts is the last word of the historical vision of the world."[2]

When this view of things pervades man's thinking, he is bound to conceive of the church in categories drawn from sociology, social psychology, and empirical observation. Churches are fellowships of believers, and the constituents of fellowship are exclusively human. Churches are social institutions, and the effect of their work can be measured by objective yardsticks. The projects in which the church engages are chosen by its members and determined by their ideas of what is at once desirable and possible. These projects and programs are evaluated in much the same way as those of the Community Fund or the Rotary Club. The length of the church and its breadth lie easily within the reach of finite yardsticks.

With this stock of implicit assumptions, we may encounter little difficulty in adopting some of the phrases which the apostles used in speaking of the church—the church as a fellowship of believers or as the congregation of the faithful. But difficulties appear when we encounter other descriptions such as

---

[2] M. Eliade, *The Myth of the Eternal Return,* New York: Pantheon Press, 1954.

"elect exiles of the dispersion," "the body of Christ," "the temple of God." In fact, we have difficulty wherever a description of the church affirms its heavenly origin and destiny.

Contemporary thinking about the church is embarrassed by these terms. They are opaque. They appear to be enemies of comprehension rather than essential tools. And let us be quite frank. They *are* enemies of comprehension so long as we remain unconcerned with the heavenly dimensions of the Church. They are essential tools of comprehension only if our concern is with the mystery of the Church's being, with God's plan for the Church's mission to principalities and powers in heavenly places, with the activity of the living Christ and the Holy Spirit in bringing redemption and reconciliation to those whose names are written in heaven.

Whenever the activity of God is drawn into the description of the church, or of anything else in fact, this description is bound to be labeled mythological. The historicist (for so we may call the position outlined above) limits *history* to the field of human events in such a way that reference to activity by God becomes mythological. But note that it is the historicist who is first responsible for separating the historical from the mythological, as far as east from west. This radical disjunction would have been quite unintelligible to any New Testament writer. He tells each story in such a way as to show the simultaneous involvement of the heavenly and the earthly. His story about human affairs is a story in which the central actor is God, to whom the Psalmist says:

> Thy way was through the sea, . . .
>     yet thy footprints were unseen
>
> —Psalm 77:19

Biblical narratives will necessarily be more mythological than any historian will tolerate whose method and assumptions exclude a living, acting God. But by the same token, they will be more historical than any myth-maker will tolerate whose method and assumptions reject temporal earthly happenings as a stage fit for the gods.

## THE CHURCH IN GOD'S WARFARE

We now shift our attention to a specific product of "mythological" imagination: the church as God's army. God is pictured throughout the New Testament as engaged in an all-out effort to evict Satan, who is the prince of the power of the air and ruler of the kingdom of darkness. He sent the Messiah as a decisive leader in this conflict, a warrior King to struggle with and overcome the rulers of this age. This King began his ministry by an encounter with the evil one in the wilderness of temptation. His victory here revealed the defeat of Satan in heaven, and enabled him to unmask and defeat the demons who harass man. He proclaimed that he came not to bring peace, but a sword. He enlisted soldiers for the struggle and required of them a radical and total renunciation of their ties to the enemy. He made it clear that they must participate in this struggle as fully as he, under his authority, subject to his commands, and bound to his defeat and victory. A king, he taught, does not declare war unless he is willing to pay the costs of victory. To his enlistees he issues suitable armor for this struggle. He teaches them a prayer for the battle: "deliver us from the evil one." He instructs them on how to carry on the battle, not with "flesh and blood," but with the rulers in the heavenly places. Both he and they have but one objective: universal and cosmic triumph—earthly, heavenly, immediate, ultimate. The stakes in this warfare are so high that every episode in their battle with the adversary has tremendous import—victory or defeat for Christ or for the devil. Yet they do not wage their campaigns in blind uncertainty of the outcome. The gates of Hades will not prevail against them, even though preliminary skirmishes may fully demonstrate the wiles and power of their adversary. Faith in him and reliance upon his methods and armament make them as a colony of heaven quite invincible. The church has authority on earth because this authority has been issued from heaven. The purpose of this authority is to free men from the slavery which the demonic forces have established on earth.

We need not, I think, argue that this view of things is dominated by mythological modes of perception. But we need to stress the fact that this pattern of thought is equally and simultaneously historical. The basic lines of the struggle for power are those which govern the story of Jesus from baptism in the Jordan to the completion of that baptism on Golgotha. From the standpoint of the community of believers, the same struggle permeates the ordinary daily life of the church, for on every hand it encounters temptations and trials similar to those of its Lord. The church is aware that Satan roams about as a lion seeking someone to devour.

No matter how alienated we may be from this mode of thinking we should recognize that if this be myth, it is a myth that has been radically historicized, demythologized, and made thoroughly existential. And if this be history, it is history that has been radically mythologized, because every event is seen as marking the convergence and divergence of divine and human wills. In any case, two affirmations are undoubtedly true of New Testament thinking about the church:

1. The church traces its origins and its vital energies to strategic events in heaven, where God has declared war on his Satanic Majesty and has demonstrated the mode and tools of final victory.

2. God has called the church to serve as his army in this cosmic battle with the devil, a battle which proceeds simultaneously on earth and in heaven. If these be mythological, then we must make the best of it.

## WEAPONS OF WARFARE

Let us now select two aspects of this warfare for closer examination: the weapons which are effective, and the prayer which

is appropriate. As to the matter of arms, no more complete cata-
log may be found than in the sixth chapter of Ephesians.

> Your loins girt with truth
> The breastplate of righteousness
> Feet shod with . . . the gospel of peace
> The shield of faith
> The helmet of salvation
> The sword of the Spirit

Ordinarily, I suppose, we misread this passage in two ways. We
turn logistic commands into moralistic advice. And we assume
that the advice is addressed to individual Christians in order to
improve their character. Exhortations are, of course, included,
but the basis for the exhortations should not be overlooked. And
both the indicatives and the imperatives are addressed to the
Christian community, and to individuals only as members of the
army of Christ.

The ultimate adversaries in the war are clearly identified:
God and the devil.

> We are not contending against flesh and blood,
> but against the principalities, against the
> powers, against the world rulers of this pres-
> ent darkness, against the spiritual hosts of
> wickedness in the heavenly places. (6:12.)

There is a finality about this conflict: it is "the evil day," the
day when spiritual forces have set themselves the objective of
destroying God's army. In this day, to stand unshakable is itself a tremendous victory.

But what kind of battlefield do we visualize—some situation of
dramatic earth-shaking significance which attracts a crowd of
reporters, photographers, and souvenir-seekers? Not at all. The
situations visualized in Ephesians seem entirely out of line with
this grandiose terminology of "evil day" and "the spiritual hosts
of wickedness." How do parents and children treat one another
at home? (6:1-4) With what motives and attitudes do masters

and slaves carry on their daily chores? (6:5-9) These are segments of the front line where victories and defeats are registered.
Here is where the strength of the Lord and the whole armor of
God are needed if the wiles of the devil are to be met success-
fully. Each parent and child, each master and slave, as "servants of Christ," deals at the source of passion or apathy with
principalities and powers. By standing "in the Lord" and living
"to the Lord" each soldier demonstrates his solidarity with the
whole army.

Because the conflict has this abysmal ground, this cosmic
scope, and these superhuman adversaries, it should be obvious
that ordinary earthly armament is entirely useless. To be sure,
analogies are drawn from the typical Roman soldier's equipment:
armor, breastplate, helmet, sword. But the actual fighting tools
are of another order entirely: the gospel of peace, for example,
or the word of God. For a situation viewed as total war, such
weapons seem pathetically inadequate. Yet this very disparity
between situation and weapons may be an intentional way of
reminding the army of the folly of its gospel: a suffering Messiah, a kingdom recruited from lepers and harlots, the powerless-
ness of Pilate before the power of his prisoner, the eternal covenant sealed by a piece of bread and a sip of wine.

What makes such weapons appropriate to this warfare is the
fact that by his work among men Jesus had turned all ideas of
warfare completely upside down. To be sure, his was a final
warfare, but it defies our usual pictures of the struggle for power
—international, ethical, psychological, or cultural. To call it
war seems fantastic because the various forms of earthly conflict are considered to be so much more tangible or terrible, more
heroic or catastrophic. The efforts of capitalist society to defeat communist society, for example, much more obviously de-
serve the name war, whether hot or cold. But to the early
Christians the conflict with principalities and powers, although
more subtle and baffling, was even more dramatic, because it
was more decisive, and yet the very decisiveness was entirely
inconspicuous. They realized that in such a conflict the armor

of God was not only necessary, but also bound to be scorned and derided by those who derived their measurements of power from the devil rather than from the mystery of salvation.

This scorn and derision was, of course no danger to the Christian community except as it invaded their own hearts. If they should begin to laugh at the absurdity of believing that a master's brutality to his slave was a greater defeat than Jerusalem suffered at the hands of Vespasian, or at the absurdity of believing that a father who provoked his children to anger was but demonstrating the victory of the devil—if they should laugh at these ideas as being preposterous, then the game was truly up. The "flaming darts of the evil one" would have reached the target. This was why a particular kind of shield was so efficacious—the shield of faith. Without this shield there was no hope, because the very battle would have been conceded before it began; that is, a false conception of which battles are significant would have won the field. Only if the cosmic spiritual warfare is the true state of affairs does faith serve as a shield at all. And unless this cosmic spiritual warfare were being fought on the intimate, invisible field of human hearts, this shield would be quite useless. But in a world where God's power operates supremely through the weakness of a Man, perhaps man's inveterate effort to define God's power in more impressive ways does represent an ultimate enemy. If that is true, then the climax of the list of "arms" in Ephesians makes sense.

> Pray at all times in the Spirit, with all prayer and
> supplication . . . for all the saints, and also for me. ( 6:
> 18-19.)

To the writer of those lines, prayer—and especially intercessory prayer—could be a weapon of the greatest power. If this isn't true for us, then it must be because our analysis of the military situation is different. But to the extent that we locate the only genuine drama in the depths of faith's struggle, to that same extent our grasp of the significance of intercessory prayer will grow.

## PRAYER AS A WEAPON

Let us look then at the prayer which the church has adopted as specially appropriate for its peculiar warfare. I have in mind here the familiar *Our Father*. Let us see whether it is too bizarre to think of this as the church's prayer for battle.

A first comment on the prayer is this: it seems utterly remote from a battle prayer, because it presupposes the weakness of the petitioners. Of ourselves, it seems to say, we cannot count even on daily bread, not to mention the forgiveness of trespasses, the power to avoid temptation, or the strength to overcome evil. Apart from God we can do nothing. We are, in fact, those in whose weakness God's strength may be displayed. This prayer itself breathes a total lack of self-assurance, self-determination, and self-reliance.

A second observation, often overlooked, is this: the prayer presupposes the close unity of the family which prays. It is *our*, not *my*, Father whom we ask to forgive *us* and not *me*. The term "Father" assumes a community of sons. In the New Testament those who are his sons constitute the *Church*. Moreover, Israel is addressed by God throughout the Bible as "my Son." When Jesus taught this prayer, he taught it to the twelve disciples who almost certainly represent the twelve tribes of Israel. It is assumed that the prayer belonged to the people of the covenant and that it expressed their dependence on the God who had created them as a people.

Now we shall reflect on the meaning of the petition: "Thy will be done, on earth as it is in heaven." For the early Christians there were many implications here which slip by unless we are alert to them. To be specific, this petition implies that before God's will can be done on earth it must have been done in the heavens. And if it has been done in the heavens, then the one who prays knows the virtual certainty of an appropriate sequel on earth. But God's particular will (God is always a person whose will is embodied in specific purposes and specific actions) has not always triumphed in heaven. The one who prays has just heard or seen that a particular purpose has at last been realized in heaven. But not yet has the corresponding event taken place on earth. Yet this *can* now take place, in fact, it *must* now take place, since it has been begun in heaven. And to its taking place on earth, the use of the petition is not irrelevant.

But what has specifically happened in heaven as Jesus saw it? How had God's will been accomplished there? We cannot, of course, give a detailed and certain answer, but perhaps the clue may be given in the cry "thy kingdom come. . . ." God's kingdom has now come in heaven. The authority of God has been re-instituted over the devil—in heaven. Jesus has seen Satan fallen from heaven. (Luke 10:18.) "The accuser of our brethren has been thrown down." (Revelations 12:10.) This is news of the first order—a report from the battlefield where a decisive encounter has been concluded. It is those whose wills have been magnetized by this victory who are impelled to beg that what has been realized in heaven may be extended to earth.

Interpreted in this fashion, the prayer for the kingdom's coming places the praying church within the context of a very definite wartime situation. The community is aware of a time lapse between the coming of God's kingdom in the heavens and the extension of that same kingdom over the earth. The kingdom has been set in motion, is coming toward us, is at the very doors. It is as close to men as God's heavenly action is close to his earthly action. The church knows now that it can come. More than that, the family of God knows that it *will* come, and that it *must* come.[3]

There is an order of divine necessity and election, of divine determination and independence, but this order is apparent only to the men whose wills are being expressed in such petitions as this, "thy kingdom come." The powers of the kingdom move into the earthly scene through the actual victories which God wins over Satan on human battlefields. And prayer is an essential accompaniment and expression of this movement. He who

---

[3]We will examine this element more fully in Chapter Four.

prays for the extension of the kingdom from heaven to earth confesses by his prayer that his will has been captured by the heavenly Victor. His prayer is an act of receptive power, an act by which he welcomes the kingdom of the heavenly Victor into his own segment of earthly territory. Seen in this light, the prayer is no mere psychological exercise, no puny effort at self-salvation, no exercise in mystical introspection, no effort for mental poise, but a mythological act, an event marking a real shift in the battle, an event where heaven joins earth in a battle which pervades both.

This wartime imagery throws fresh light upon the implications of life in that family which can pray so confidently: *Our Father.* Only as newborn babes are they moved to call God "Father." It is as joint heirs with Christ that sonship is theirs. (Romans 8:14-17; Galatians 4:4-7; 1 Peter 1:17, 18, 23; 2:3). The event of rebirth is a genuine event—something decisive has happened in the primordial heights and depths. And this event has a genuinely communal dimension; each son says "we." The address of prayers to the Father is the celebration of a family's coming into existence. In the same sense in which God's kingdom has recently been inaugurated in the heavens with the eviction of Satan, God has become our Father and we his sons, and this event has transpired in the heavens. Our sonship, our adoption has actually taken place. We have been born again, born from above. And our prayer springs out of this radically new situation. We as sons address our father with reference to the next step in his plan—the further transference of this victory from heaven to earth. The true community, where God is truly our Father, has been realized in the heavens. Naturally, then, this family eagerly awaits its extension on earth.

Now even so simple a thing as daily rations becomes a matter related to the wider warfare. Members of the army likewise recognize that the forgiveness of daily sins is itself a sign of the Messiah's power and of the kingdom's nearness. The prayer for forgiveness is therefore an act of forgiveness, since man's reconciliation to God in heaven cannot be separated from reconciliation to enemies on earth.

Most clearly of all do the needs of the army in warfare determine the shape of the prayer in the petition "Deliver us from the *evil one.*" No, that is not a garbled text. Almost all scholars agree that the phrase is not "from evil" but "from the evil one," that is from Satan, our most deceptive adversary. In this petition, therefore, what is implicit in the rest of the prayer becomes quite explicit. A state of war exists between God and Satan. The one who prays, "as God's soldier, is constantly exposed to the attacks of the devil and must therefore be watchful and armed at his post."[4] The plea to be spared from temptation refers to the danger of falling before Satan's attack. The company of soldiers begs their Commander, in effect, "Let us not come into the attack, into the danger of falling, but tear us out of the power of Satan."[4] This company stands on the very battle line. They are praying in the very moment of battle. This is the place and time where the kingdom which has come in heaven is pressing forward to its coming on earth. Satan uses every subterfuge to prevent that coming. If he succeeds in destroying the faith of God's army, then God's kingdom falls short of full earthly actualization. But if the army's prayer is answered, their deliverance from the evil one will mark God's manifest power, a strategic shift in power along the whole line of battle. In short, the act of praying becomes a weapon through which God's might is released against Satan. To the extent, then, that the church's life may be described in military language, to that extent the Lord's Prayer takes on its full meaning as a battle prayer.

## THE FRONTIER IN THIS WARFARE

Wherever, then, we touch the New Testament conception of the horizons of the church, we are confronted with a way of

[4] K. G. Kuhn, in K. Stendahl, *The Scrolls and the New Testament,* New York: Harper & Brothers, 1957, pp. 96f.
[4] *Ibid.*

thinking which gives priority at every point to the *heavenly* world, and within the heavenly world, to the powers of God's kingdom as he reclaims territory from Satan. If the church is a heavenly reality, so, too, are Satan's hordes. If the church exists in the heavens, so, too, do nations, tribes, tongues, and peoples. This being so, we must press a bit further in describing the work of the church in heaven. As there are gods many and lords many, so, too, the heavens are full of communities many. How do we, then, separate the family of Christ from all other families? The key criterion is one already suggested: which cause is being supported in creation's civil war? The mission of the church as the army of Christ is to witness by its very existence to the victory which God has won and is winning over the devil. And this witness must be delivered to principalities and powers in the heavenly places.

It is far from easy to describe in empirical, pragmatic terms what this mission to principalities and powers entailed. But the difficulty does not permit the church to restrict its assignment to an earthly crusade to secure quite tangible earthly objectives. God's army has a double assignment. (Ephesians 2:9-10.) "To make all men see what is the plan of the mystery. . . ." That is an earthly assignment. To make known "the manifold wisdom of God . . . *to the principalities and powers* in the heavenly places." That obviously is a task which reaches far beyond earthly confines. As the apostles viewed the matter, the church's mission to men was simultaneously a mission to principalities and powers, and vice versa. The two missions could not be separated, in this mythological way of viewing things, because men's wisdom and men's loyalties are a primary battleground on which "the heavenly rulers of this darkness" seek to maintain their hold.

That the church has been placed in a strategic situation for accomplishing this mission to principalities and powers is presupposed by the news which the apostle announces. Jesus Christ has been raised "far above all rule and authority and power and dominion. . . ." This means that he is head over all things and that the church is his body, his fullness. (Ephesians 1:21-23.) And God has raised the church "to sit with him in the heavenly places in Christ Jesus." (2:6.)

This mythological vision may not enable us to describe with precision the mission and the unity of the church because the description will perforce be as mythological as the reality demands which is being described. But the mythological perspective makes three conclusions quite inescapable.

1. There can be but *one* mission of this church: its inclusive and total service. A divided, broken, conflicting mission cannot be the mission of which the New Testament speaks. Where the church is engaged in its authentic assignment, it will manifest its oneness in Christ.

2. There cannot be unity in the church except in terms of the fulfillment of this mission. A unity achieved on other grounds and for other motives is not the oneness of the body, "the fullness of him who fills all in all." Whenever the oneness of the church appears, it will appear as a total obedience to the commands of Christ Jesus: "to make all men see . . . to make known to principalities and powers."

3. The unity in mission of God's army is a foretaste and an instrument of achieving the consummation of unity throughout all creation, a unity of authority and obedience, a unity of judgment and grace, a unity of heaven and earth as "a dwelling place of God in the Spirit." (2:22.)

None of us can draw, in terms of its empirical earthly form, the shape of this one church. Its horizons are too vast and too near at hand for that. But we can be sure that its shape is that of an embassy from heaven to earth. The direction and demands of this mission derive from the perennially new revelation to us in Christ Jesus of the heights and depths of God's redeeming power, for our wrestling is not with flesh and blood but with "the spiritual armies of wickedness in the heavenly places." Because Jesus Christ carried out his errand in the form of a servant, the church, too, is bound to this form. Its life is derived from the life of this particular servant, a messiah servant, in

whose obedience men may see the final humiliation and exaltation, the final defeat and victory.  Or, to shift the image, only
the slain Lamb qualifies as this army's commander-in-chief.  It
was the event of his obedience—perhaps the only event which
can be called the ontologically true event—which transformed
the balance of power in heaven and thereby makes possible a
shift in the balance of power on earth.  The depths and heights
of the church's death-and-life therefore will always correspond
to the depths and heights of the Messiah's death-and-life.  He
enables his people to share with him the heavenly places, the
heavenly conflict and victory.  Only so does its earthly story proclaim what prophets and kings have long hoped to hear.  Its
mythological story is its eternal glory.

Chapter III

# THE CITY WHERE
# GOD DWELLS

I have not looked to the heavenly city as one does to a dream; for I have not been looking for a sort of refuge from everyday monotony and the burden of existence in some airy mirage or other. On the contrary, to me that mother-country of freedom, with all its royal majesty and heavenly splendour, is something to be seen at the very heart of earthly reality, right at the core of all the confusions and all the mischances which are, inevitably, involved in its mission to men. . . .[1]

—HENRI DE LUBAC

[1]From *The Splendour of the Church* by Henri de Lubac, S.J., in the translation of Michael Mason, © 1956, Sheed and Ward, Inc., New York.

We have spoken of the church as the people who inherit God's glory by living at the point where God glorifies men and men glorify God. Such a manner of speaking is, of course, virtually meaningless except for men who have beheld God's glory both in the face of human persons and in the fabric of human community. When glory is recognized as an essential constituent of one particular community, then other communities will be measured by whether or not they embody this glory. God's glory irradiates that city wherein he dwells.

We have also been thinking of the church as an army of God through which God promotes on earth his warfare with heavenly antagonists. We have tried to expound the military vocabulary of the New Testament, and this has required the use of a mythological idiom. In the New Testament these military terms often coalesce with political images. For example, in Philippians 3:20, the army has its capital city in which it holds its citizenship. For this city it fights. Toward this city it longs to march. Both doxological and mythological contexts lead us to the point of considering the church as the city of God.

In many passages of the New Testament the city of God is quite specifically named. It is not just any metropolitan area, not an anonymous never-never town, but one particular city: Jerusalem. This name bears, of course, mythological and doxological meanings, but it nonetheless transmits particular historical associations, and it is our objective now to call attention to this circle of associations.

It needs little demonstration, I think, to suggest that these meanings, whatever they may be, are almost totally dormant in contemporary Protestant minds. If any bells ring when this rope is pulled, they ring very, very softly. To be sure, there is a modern body which calls itself "The Church of the New Jerusalem." No doubt for its members this title preserves the rich colors of ancient tapestries but for most of us there can be only a faded, musty archaism in such a name. Reminders of this vanished metropolis come only through occasional hymns or scripture lessons, or at a burial service. Although city-bred and city-distracted, we rarely think of the church as a city. And even though we are loyal to some city where we have resided the longest or where the home ties are strongest, not many of us really want to live in Jerusalem, however renovated. Our minds seldom link our church to Jerusalem because this city does not really exist for us.

Our insensitivity in this area marks a huge distance between us and the ancients, for to them the religious character of the city was axiomatic. In one sense, every city was a holy sanctuary to both Greeks and Romans because it was an abode common to gods and men. In establishing a city, the setting up of an altar was essential, for worship formed the cohesive power of community. A city was built to be eternal. So Livy could write, "There is not a place in this city which is not impregnated with religion and which is not occupied by some divinity. The Gods inhabit it."[2]

Even more prominently than in Greece and Rome, the Oriental kingdoms expressed in their myths the centrality of the city. Every important city was created according to a celestial arche-

---

[2] cf. Fustel de Coulanges, *The Ancient City*, New York, 1956, pp. 140-146.

type. This celestial city forms the very center of ultimate reality. The earthly city participates in the symbolic ultimacy of its celestial counterpart. Here the center of the earth is linked most closely to the center of heaven. The mountain in the city and the temple on the mountain thus become the symbolic meeting point of heaven, earth, and hell.[3]

It is therefore not surprising to find among Jewish writings of the New Testament period or earlier the development of a pattern of archetypal thinking about Jerusalem. Thus, for example, God had prepared a heavenly Jerusalem which he had showed Adam before he sinned. (2 Baruch 4:2-7.) The earthly Jerusalem derived its reality and importance from its relationship to its celestial counterpart. It was the navel of the earth, the point where creation began and where Adam had been formed.[4] The Jerusalem which is now above is the Holy City which will soon appear. "Then shall the city that is now invisible appear." (4 Ezra 7:26.) The promise of God to the faithful is citizenship in this coming city. "For you is opened Paradise, planted the tree of life, . . . a city builded, a rest appointed." (4 Ezra 8:52.)

So, too, early Christians thought of their community as the Holy City, Jerusalem, and this thought articulated a sense of kinship simultaneously to the Jerusalem that is above, the Jerusalem that is to come, and the Jerusalem on earth, the city of David, site of the sacred mountain and the temple.

## TYPOLOGY

If we are to comprehend the horizons of their life as a community, therefore, we must explore this web of relations. This exploration plunges us immediately into what is technically called typology, a mode of perception which is difficult to adopt and even more difficult to control. Americans who are acquainted with the varied typologies in the Bible are almost unanimously repelled by them. And who wouldn't be struck by the

[3]cf. Eliade, *op. cit.*, p. 12.
[4]Eliade, *op. cit.*, p. 16f.

fantastic in some of them? For example, the sign of Jonah is
seen to lie in the fact that as Jonah spent three days in the
whale's belly, so would Jesus spend three days in the bowels of
the earth. (Matthew 12:39-40.) Again, in 1 Peter, a significant
analogy is described between Christian baptism and Noah's
building of the ark. (1 Peter 3:20-21.) Or again, in John, the
bread of the Eucharist is like, yet also unlike, the manna eaten
by Israel in the wilderness wandering. (John 6:49-50.) Or
finally, the blood of Jesus is seen to be typologically related to
the blood of Abel. (Hebrews 12:24.) Such comparisons fall far
short of sense. It is tempting, therefore, to dismiss all typologies
because so many of them are intolerably bizarre. But theologians and historians are discovering that it is not so easy to
jettison all use of typology, whether in biblical tradition or in
our own modern habits of thought.

It becomes increasingly impossible, for example, to describe
the person and work of Jesus Christ without comparing him to
his predecessors in Israel. The New Testament links him to
Adam, Isaac, Joseph, Moses, Aaron, David, Elijah, Jeremiah—and
this is but a partial list. Each of these links is typological in
nature.

In a similar way early Christians described their communal
solidarity in terms of typological correspondences with the past.
They were sons of Adam and sons of Abraham. They were the
twelve tribes of Israel, over which the twelve apostles had been
chosen to rule. They were exiles from Egypt, painfully making
their way to the Promised Land, celebrating the feast of un-
leavened bread and the unblemished lamb. And finally, they
were citizens of the Holy City, the new Jerusalem. What were
they trying to convey through this welter of types? An answer
to this question depends, first of all, upon our understanding
and evaluating this kind of description. Just what constitutes
typology?

We should be clear at the outset that typology is a form of
mythological thinking in which there may be a seriously ontological thrust; that is, by typology, men attempt to communicate

their conviction about ultimate reality. They give expression to the conviction that the invisible realm is not only utterly real but also the ground of existence for the visible realm. To be sure, it is possible to limit one's sense of the real to the visible. An atheist has been defined as a man without any invisible means of support. An atheistic community, likewise, assumes that it lives without invisible means of support. But the great mythologies of the ancient world articulate the conviction that such atheism is an illusion. The mythologies voiced the assurance that human society derives its support from some invisible reality, and that this invisible reality determines the empirical forms. Every earthly community has its heavenly original. Communities which have no connection to this original, this pattern in the purpose of God, have no genuinely durable significance. Each contemporary community is related to a "double" which is at once prior and higher than itself, a heavenly counterpart which is the creative source and objective standard of the visible phenomenon. The heavenly city exerts a primal force, takes a prominent initiative, and gives some degree of permanence to cities which represent it. "Neither the objects of the external world nor human acts, properly speaking, have any autonomous intrinsic value. Objects or acts acquire a value, and in so doing become real, because they participate . . . in a reality that transcends them."[5]

The next axiom of the typological viewpoint is this: two or more empirical structures which are related to the same heavenly original are thereby related to each other. Flowing from the same source they are comparable, yet different, embodiments of that source. If their original is essential to God's eternal purpose, the comparison of the earthly types (sometimes distinguished as antitype and type) is called for by their interdependence.

Typology, therefore, is an analogical form of thinking and speaking which focuses attention upon two or more pivotal realities (e.g., Adam and Christ) and in so doing apprehends the hidden connection between those realities and their common source. It thereby simultaneously apprehends the connection, also hidden, between those realities and other earthly phenomena. Beginning with this definition, we may specify six features which characterize biblical typology.

1. Typology is prompted by a concern to understand what has happened and what is happening. It is a way of dealing with specific communities or persons within temporality. Typology is concerned *not* so much with words or texts in Scripture, as with the communities or persons about whom the story centers. This distinguishes typology from both parable and allegory. Jerusalem always refers to people who are bound together by residence in a specific historical community.

A contrast to the prevailing temper of the New Testament is provided by Philo.

> Now the city of God is called in the Hebrew Jerusalem and its name when translated is vision of peace. Therefore do not seek the city of the Existent among the regions of the earth . . . but in a soul in which there is no warring, whose sight is keen, which has set before it as its aim to live in contemplation and peace.[6]

2. Typology is concerned with invisible but real connections between two or more persons or communities. The New Jerusalem has many links to the old, and these links are essential to the life of both communities because they determine their ultimate status. The connections are actually there, but they are imbedded so deeply in the invisible history from which both communities spring that no causal, temporal, or speculative analysis can uncover them. A connection is affirmed because both communities "are vertically linked to Divine Providence, which alone is able to devise such a plan of history and supply the key to its understanding."[7] The connection itself, though

---

[6] De Somn. 2:250. I am indebted to C. K. Barrett for this translation.

[7] E. Auerbach, *Mimesis*, New Jersey: Princeton University Press, 1953, p. 74.

grasped by analogy, is believed to have a genuine ground in ultimate Being. The connection is affirmed at the deepest conceivable level—the eternal purposes of the eternal God. The temporal cities need not manifest externally what it is which binds them together, and in fact do not do so. It is because the archetypal city is at work in both earthly cities that the two are related. Therefore each community has significance for the other. The first prefigures, anticipates, or promises the second. The second includes, fufills, and moves beyond the first. The distinction between the two indicates a temporal distance. They both happened once-upon-a-time, and not at the same time. Yet their mutual relationship to God's purpose gives them a rootage in what lies before and after the times. The city which Adam saw before his sin is the same city which will appear at the end of the ages.

3. Each of the earthly cities is representative of many visible communities. Although each city is a particular, once-upon-a-time phenomenon, yet neither city can be bounded by lines drawn on a map. What happened "once-upon-a-time" has happened "once-for-all-time" and has happened for us. Some of us cannot grasp this mode of thought as easily in the case of cities as in the case of the Adam-Christ typology.[8] He who is "in Christ" or "in Adam" is bound to the Eternal through these corporate personalities. He participates in the events narrated about Adam and Christ without destroying their once-for-all character. The later event is conceived as present in some sense with the earlier, and the interpreter who views them both becomes contemporaneous with both.

Thus the two-point analogy becomes a three-point analogy, "Adam-Christ-ourselves." The analogy then comes to express the true and ultimate status of all men.

> The doctrine becomes intelligible when Adam, and when Christ, are understood not as atomically distinct beings but

---

[8] cf. E. Best, *One Body in Christ*, London, 1955. p. 41.

as truly participating in the essence of all mankind and as epitomizing that essence in themselves.[9]

Many of us find profound meanings in the fact of our own membership in Adam's body of sin-and-death and in Christ's body of righteousness-and-life.[10] But we have not yet begun to apply the same modes of thought to our citizenship in the two Jerusalems. Yet the same kind of thinking is applicable here. We are citizens of the Holy City; as citizens of the new Jerusalem, we belong as well to the Jerusalem of the old covenant. If this were not so, the city of David and Solomon, the city of Jeremiah and Ezekiel, would always remain a foreign country to us. Fellowship in the church links us to the heavenly Jerusalem and through this city to the City of David.

4. The act of seeing and recounting the inner connections between the two cities of the biblical saga is simultaneously an act of making clear the involvement of present choices in that saga. When the prophet has revealed to us the contemporary reality of the two cities, this revelation forces upon us the choice of loyalty to one or the other commonwealth. This impels us to recognize inwardly our own solidarity with the communities of whom the story is told. Authentic typology indicates an action of the Holy Spirit in the storyteller, an action which relates the prophet to his audience and which also relates both prophet and audience to the God who was at work in Jerusalem. This storyteller thus becomes more than a yarn spinner. He is himself existentially involved in the ultimate questions posed by the existence of the two cities.

5. Because typological thought represents spiritual activity on the part of one who perceives a divine purpose linking two separate communities, it follows that it is his reflection upon his citizenship in the second and later city, the *new* Jerusalem, which reveals its kinship to its prototype. Only those who are sons of Abraham through faith can discern their relationship to

---

[9]Philip Wheelright, *The Burning Fountain,* Indiana:　Indiana University Press. p. 161. Used by permission.

[10]cf. K. Barth, *Christ and Adam,* New York, 1957.

the sons of Abraham by the flesh. Only those who perceive oneness in the body of Christ can perceive their oneness in the body of Adam.[11] Likewise it is awareness of his citizenship in the new Jerusalem which impels the Christian prophet to retell the stories of the older city. In this sense, the genesis of typological reflection is to be found in the baptized memory of a reborn community.

6. Biblical typology, however, has a strong orientation toward the future. There is an implicit eschatology in the ways in which New Testament writers used typology. Paul as typologist is a prophetic figure, who reveals to his churches the destiny to which in Adam and in Christ they are foreknown. In other words, he tells the story of the two Adams in order to make clear how the future impends on the present. Adam is the prefiguration not only of Christ but also of me in my sin and mortality. In him I look forward to God's faithful judgment, just as in Christ I look forward to the mercy which lies behind and beyond the sin and death of Adam. So, too, citizens of the new Jerusalem look forward toward a city which is to come.[12]

New Testament typology is eschatological in still another sense. We recall that typologies, like all metaphors, combine similarities *and* contrasts. The old city and the new are both alike and unlike. The similarity of the two Jerusalems stresses the continuity of God's action in both. The discontinuity appears at the point where the new city completes, fulfills, replaces, and even destroys the old. The prophet who is like Moses is not only a second Moses, but one in whom the Mosaic law finds its true end. The Church as Israel is continuous with the story of the patriarchs, but *this Israel* is the end as well as the vindication of the promise to the patriarchs. The correspondence underscores the contrast. And both together witness to a real movement forward toward the actualization of God's intention for mankind. Biblical typology as a mode of thought is distinct both from a purely cyclical view of history and from a

---

[11]cf. Barth, *op. cit.*, p. 33f.
[12]cf. Phil. 3:20.

purely linear view as well. It expresses a sense of progress through God's providential fulfillment of his promise, a fulfillment in which the new city links its citizens simultaneously to the heavenly reality and to the coming earthly reality.

Thus far in this chapter we have tried chiefly to recapture the basic ingredients of typology as a mode of thought, and to illustrate these ingredients in terms of the New Jerusalem. We now turn to specific writers in the New Testament with the query: What may we learn about the church from their descriptions of it as the new Jerusalem, the Holy City?

## JOHN'S VISION OF JERUSALEM

We begin with John's prophecy in the Book of Revelation. We should not forget that by the time John was imprisoned on Patmos the capital of Judea had already lain in ruins twenty-five years. There was a minimum of external similarity between the churches in Laodicea or Philadelphia and the city on the Judean hills. And there was a minimum of sentimental attachment as well. The Gentiles of Asia would have considered the geographical Jerusalem wholly undesirable as a place of residence. So surprising it is to visualize Gentile Christians as welcoming inclusion in the Holy City, that some scholars cannot accept the thesis that the Book of Revelation was addressed to them.[13]  But the historical evidence is quite overwhelming that the churches in Asia were predominantly Gentile. Doubly significant it is, therefore, that in writing to them, John should appeal to this promise from their living Lord: "He who conquers, I will make him a pillar in the temple of my God; never shall he go out of it, and I will write on him the name of my God, and the name of the city of my God, the New Jerusalem which comes down from my God out of heaven, and my own new name." (Revelation 3:12.)

What does such a promise suggest as to the view of the church? Among the obvious inferences are these: Jerusalem

---

[13]cf. S. G. F. Brandon *The Fall of Jerusalem*, London, 1951, pp. 182ff.

is the name of God's city, the community which he has designed for his own possession, where he dwells in a unique way. Personal destiny is unthinkable apart from the establishment of this community. The disciple who conquers receives not only a new name to accord with his reborn self but also a name which fits his new community. There is in fact but *one name* for each person who conquers. That name is simultaneously the *name of God, the name of Christ,* and *the name of the city* which comes down from God. This is the supreme reward for "patient endurance"; in "conquering," the victor walks straight through the open door into God's own city (3:8-12).

This city has an inner history of its own, with its own traditions and culture, its own boundaries and polity. In some decisive way it is *like* the Jerusalem of Judea; but it is the *New* Jerusalem, and therefore in some decisive ways unlike the Judean hill town. The site of this community is determined not by geography, but by the location of God's temple; it is situated where God dwells. Its time is not determined by the calendar, but by Christ's promise and the church's response. Whenever and wherever a Christian congregation conquers, there and then the descent of the new Jerusalem is manifested in that victory. Obedient *to* Christ they share in the obedience *of* Christ and therefore share in his name; sharing in his name they share in his city; and because his obedience was totally directed to God, this city is none other than God's city, the place of his abiding.[14]

Whenever and wherever this happens, God reveals the hidden lineage between this new city and its earthly predecessor. The city of the Son of David *is* the city of David. The new temple is a continuation of both the tent of meeting in the wilderness and the temple of Solomon. Mount Zion in the heart of the new city is the old Mount Zion.

In other visions the prophet develops these allegorical similarities. Both cities have foundations: walls, gates, trees, water (chapters 21 and 22). Both are the residence of the people of

---

[14]cf. L. S. Thornton, *Christ and the Church*, London, 1956, pp. 32-44.

God. Both are illuminated by God's glory. God's people need not try proudly to prove their superiority over past generations or over other cities; they need only to acknowledge their oneness with those generations and cities by glorifying the same God, the same King.

At this point we must, however, speak a word of caution. Solidarity with the same holy city does not require an indiscriminate romanticizing of the Jerusalem of prophetic lore and cultic saga. The very prophet who calls the holy city "Jerusalem" speaks as well of Jerusalem as the city where Jesus was crucified. This very city (the place on the map) is even called Sodom and Egypt! Or again, the prophet can associate Jerusalem with Babylon, the mother of harlots! In short, the city of God and the city of Satan cannot be separated by geographical limits. The line between them follows the contours of *gloria dei* vs. *gloria mundi*, or the contours of the battle line in God's warfare with Satan. And the clearest boundary marker may be seen in the obedience of Jesus unto death and in the corresponding obedience of his witnesses. (Revelation 12:10-12.) To belong to him is to belong to the celestial commonwealth which is known by its descent to earth. And citizenship in this realm links the citizen simultaneously to the old Jerusalem through the new, for the new community is one where God's promises to the old and the hope of the old are fulfilled. For example, in the new city there is no need for temple buildings because God and the Lamb are there. (21:22.) There is no need of sun or moon because the glory of God is its light. Into it the kings bring the glory and honor of the nations. Here the people of God reign forever in total and final sovereignty. The new mountain with its temple is made entirely movable. All generations in all countries now have access to it. They have access here and now to the Jerusalem which is above, to the original and to the coming Jerusalem.

Here, if you will, is the prophet's answer to various questions concerning the horizons of the Christian society. This society is heir both of the entire past and of the entire future. It has its own orderly structure, with its own foundations, walls, gates, and glory. It is the bride of Christ, ever new, ever coming down from heaven, ever the fulfillment of God's quest for man and man's quest for God. It exists in space yet it cannot be located on the map. It has its own time, yet this time cannot be limited by the calendar. It lives in the present, yet maintains eternal solidarity with both patriarchs and apostles. It remains wholly involved in present earthly conflict with Babylon, yet it mediates in terms of that warfare the conquering and glorious power of God. No community is more "down to earth" than this, because it is the place where the holy city descends from heaven to Smyrna and Pergamum, and because this descent coincides with fully human decisions of loyalty or treason. Here are unique dimensions—height and depth, breadth and length. Can we comprehend them? If not, it may be because our hearts have no room within them for "the highways to Zion." (Psalm 84:5.)

## SINAI AND MOUNT ZION

We have been dealing thus far with the idea of the Holy City in the Book of Revelation. Now we note a similar use of typology in the Epistle to the Hebrews.

> You have come to Mount Zion and to the city of the living God, the heavenly Jerusalem, and to innumerable angels in festal gathering, and to the assembly of the first-born who are enrolled in heaven, and to a judge who is God of all, and to the spirits of just men made perfect, and to Jesus, the mediator of a new covenant, and to the sprinkled blood that speaks more graciously than the blood of Abel. (12:22-24.)

Here as in Revelation the city is pre-eminently the city of the living God. No less than in Revelation is this a heavenly city, yet no less is this a city with which earth's denizens have direct contact. "You have come to Mount Zion." As in Revelation the holy city is heralded as the place where earth and heaven

meet, the point where men and God stand nearest to each other.
This meeting is an assembly for worship, with its fear and
trembling, its confession and remission of sins. This worship
unites the earthly congregation with the cloud of witnesses and
with the community of angels, gathered in festival joy and
praise. (12:24.) Here men meet the Judge in fellowship with
all the "first-born," all who have been saved by grace. The
liturgical reference of these ideas is quite clear; the life of the
church is focused in worship.

It is also obvious that the author views this worship in awe-
some and even terrifying proportions. Participation in the
liturgy involves the congregation in nothing less than a cosmic
earthquake. It stands near the place where both heaven and
earth pass through the fires of final judgment. However solid
and secure both may seem, they are in reality ephemeral. An
earthquake marks their removal. But at the heart of the earthquake, the holy community shares in a realm that cannot be
shaken. It is a kingdom given to men as their only abiding
place. True liturgy makes this society vulnerable to God's judgment and yet as invulnerable as Mount Zion. (12:25-29.)

Participation in a liturgy which centers in a single covenant
sacrifice also establishes the solidarity of all generations in this
one city. The vast cloud of witnesses, the long list of heroes and
martyrs from Abel to the present—all are citizens of the city
toward which they have all journeyed, en route through the
wilderness. Because, during all the centuries, this city has been
the common goal, every generation of pilgrims has given witness
to its existence by their common faith. (12:1.) This faith,
therefore, destroys invidious comparisons between ancient and
modern pilgrims.

Even so, however, there is a newness about the heavenly
Jerusalem which distinguishes the new covenant (12:24) from
the old. To be sure, the pilgrim quest continues. Like all our
predecessors, we "seek the city which is to come." (13:14.)
But this city, this kingdom, is something which has been re-

ceived, something to which we have already come. (12:22, 28.)
And this commonwealth, the heavenly Jerusalem which has come
and to which we have come, can no more be shaken. It is the
company of "the spirits of just men made perfect." (12:23.)
The difference between old and new is essentially the difference
brought about by Jesus Christ, the pioneer and perfecter of
faith. (11:39—12:2.)

According to both Hebrews and Revelation, the heavenly city
is not less real than earthly cities but more real. It is, in fact,
the ground of their reality. This is why, in both Revelation and
in Hebrews, the Christian's citizenship in the new Jerusalem is
more terrifying, more productive of dread before the consuming
fire (Hebrew 12:29) than was citizenship in the old city. Mount
Zion, as described in Hebrews, is much more fearful than the
Sinai of Moses' days. This is not strange, since citizenship in
this new city means such disciplining as Jesus received. (Hebrews 12:4-11.) To reject now the commands of him who warns
from heaven is much more disastrous than to ignore the demands
of an earthly speaker. (12:25.) The coming of the new city
from heaven is both more catastrophic and more redemptive
than the establishment of the city of David. At these central
points then, Hebrews and Revelation convey essentially the
same message. The reality of the Church derives from the
reality of the celestial community which both *is* and *is to come*.
Men come to it by patient prayer, by steadfast hope, and by
disciplined obedience. And in coming to it, they join the age-
long caravan of pilgrims. If this City were a future goal only,
and nothing more, it would be a source of endless ambition and
endless frustration—an eternal mirage in the dry desert of
history. If it were a heavenly reality, and nothing more, it
would become a disembodied ideal, so far removed from earthly
sojourners as to increase their despair of all things earthly. No,
this City can be looked for in the future with confidence only
because it already exists in an order of reality which is as certain
as the majestic power and love of God. And this reality breaks

through into earthly embodiment in the obedience of Jesus and in the perseverance of those who look to him as "the pioneer and perfecter of faith." (Hebrews 12:1-2.)[15]

## THE MESSIAH COMES TO JERUSALEM

"The pioneer and perfecter of faith"—this is one of the best characterizations of Jesus Christ. But what light does this throw upon the character of the holy city? We have already suggested an answer. On the one hand, the horizon of the church has been located in the celestial city which is to come and which, in coming, draws into its gates all who have sought its coming. On the other hand, the key to the city is held by a person, to whom faith looks back as the pioneer and to whom faith looks ahead as perfecter. Moreover, this backward and forward look applies not alone to the individual pilgrim in his lonely trek, but it applies even more aptly to the community of the Exodus. This community, preserving its tradition concerning the pioneer, exhibited keen interest in the pioneer's relationship to Jerusalem. As symptoms of this interest, we should note the role played by this city in the gospel narratives. In some of these narratives, to be sure, the thought has to do with the place on the map—and with that alone. But in other cases, the meaning requires simultaneous reference to both the typological and the geographical entity. Nor is this surprising when we recall three facts: (1) Already in the days of Jesus, Jerusalem had long been identified with the messianic consummation of Israel's long history; (2) The churches which remembered Jesus felt themselves to be nearer to the Jerusalem of the prophet's vision than to the Jerusalem of the cartographer. (3) Those who wrote and who read the Gospels were fully acquainted with the mode of thinking expressed in Hebrews and Revelation.

The Gospels assume that the Messiah must be presented in Jerusalem, that he must go to Jerusalem—both to die and to conquer. The Messiah must bring peace to her walls and her

---

[15]cf. C. K. Barrett, in W. D. Davies and D. Daube, *The Background of the New Testament and its Eschatology*, 1956, pp. 382-386.

peoples, even though they knew not the things which pertain to that peace. It was not possible for a prophet to perish outside Jerusalem nor for a Messiah to establish his throne elsewhere. He speaks in advance of the Exodus which he will make there, and of the descent of the Spirit which must begin there. The fulfillment of his mission must involve both the salvation of the city and the destruction of the city. For Jerusalem is the site of the great apostasy as truly as it is the site of the great faithfulness. This is why the messianic woes must include both the razing and the resurrection of this city. Herein lies the scandal of the gospel, translated into its impact on every earthly embodiment of God's city. The keys of the kingdom of heaven are the keys to this city, and they belong to David and to David's son who is also David's Lord. Why otherwise does the Messiah weep over Jerusalem? He is its King. At his birth all Jerusalem is troubled. (Matthew 2:3.) At his death, saints who had died were raised and "went into the holy city." (Matthew 27:53.) It is the place whence come those who reject him (Matthew 15:1) and therefore the place where he must go to suffer. (Matthew 16:21.) The temple is his, but it must be cleansed, the fig tree must be cursed, the vineyard must be given to new tenants—yet God in accomplishing these dreadful judgments ratifies his intention to dwell in this city. (Matthew 21.) The road over which the disciples accompany their Master to Jerusalem is also the road to the heavenly Jerusalem, and therefore a road on which Jesus invites all followers to travel.

In all these passages, the influence of typological thinking should be apparent. The geographical element is not ignored, but the sense is destroyed if meaning is determined by the geographical. No, Jerusalem is from first to last the city of the Great King. It is the earthly manifestation of that heavenly community which constitutes his rightful kingdom. Here proceed both the profanation and the purgation of the temple. Here the prophet may discern both bride and harlot, both the Lamb and the Beast, both the ultimate warfare and the ultimate

78        HORIZONS OF CHRISTIAN COMMUNITY

peace. The church dwells where Satan's throne is (Revelation 2:13) and where the Spirit invites the church to participate in the Messiah's victory. (2:17.) If there are ambiguities here, and there are, they are instructive ambiguities, since they throw light upon the church's continuing mission in and to the world, and upon the church's special vulnerability to God's judgment on that world.

We must draw our reflections to a close. Admittedly typology is a difficult and hazardous kind of thought. Admittedly there is much in the biblical concept of the two cities which remains either opaque or offensive. But we should not hastily reject the potential truth inherent in thinking of the church today as linked inseparably to both the city in Judea and the heavenly city. This truth may become most luminous whenever a congregation meets in genuine worship. Does a liturgical service reflect a solidarity with all Christian churches? Does it establish an unbreakable link with Jesus and the disciples in Gethsemane? Is this worship comparable with the hosannas and with the cries "Crucify him"? If the God who is worshiped, the God who comes down in judgment and healing, is the same God, does the event of his descent link this moment to his descent on Sinai, to his descent in the pillars of cloud and fire, to his epiphany to Elijah and to Isaiah, and to the final descent? To answer such questions, one does not need to neglect the contrast between a modern congregation and the company of those who slaughtered animals in the temple on Mount Zion. But the recognition of such contrasts does not cancel the prior question as to whether this congregation participates in any significant way in the life of that earlier company. And if both companies, in fact, serve the same God, the covenanting Lord of Israel, then, indeed, the questions must receive affirmative answers. The very identification of contrasts may help to accent the hidden solidarity between the prophets, the apostles, and their contemporary successors. To the extent that a contemporary church takes note of this solidarity, to that extent it will move in the direction of a recovery of mythological and typological perspectives. Or in less technical terms, it will move in the direction of setting all Christian communities within the horizons of the Jerusalem which is above, "the assembly of the first-born who are enrolled in heaven."

These horizons will immediately reduce to proper proportion those stubborn factors which alienate existing Christian communions from one another. For if we are able to recognize Abraham and Paul, despite all the differences between them, as citizens with us of the new Jerusalem, we will also be less able to deny that such disparate fellowships as the Polish National Catholic Church, the National Baptist Convention, and the Society of Friends—with all their very important differences—are embodiments of the city of God coming down from heaven. The use of typology in short may help us to rediscover the oneness of the Church as the new Jerusalem and thereby to advance toward a genuine ecumenism in time. It follows that this ecumenism in time will accelerate the rediscovery of an ecumenism in space.

# Chapter IV

# THE TIME OF
# THE CHURCH'S LIFE

The hero arrives at the trysting-place by chronological time. He waits for what seems years by psychological time—his own private clock that measures time by values and intensity. As he waits, he recalls the various happenings that led up to this fateful rendezvous by an act of memory—an emotionally charged interpretation of events. Finally, the hero greets the beloved with the pressure of all his past on the moment of his present which is itself modified by a purposiveness that thrusts toward a future big with hope.[1]

—A. Mendilow

---

[1] From *Time and the Novel,* by A. A. Mendilow.

Ecumenism in time is a phrase which is capable of signifying at least two different truths. The first of these truths is the more obvious and more easy to describe. Considering time as basically a matter of the chronological succession of the centuries, we may visualize the church as located within the brackets of time, participating in its unceasing movement and undergoing incessant changes. Ecumenism in time connotes the strange unity which persists within and through this endless fluctuation in forms. The churches of the twentieth century acknowledge their kinship with the churches of earlier centuries. Corporate memory is stacked with symbols and images of this continuity: Scripture, prayers, hymns, sacraments, the cross, the star, the cradle, the altar. And behind the symbols the churches glimpse an overarching unity in terms of the activity of the triune God, and articulate this glimpse in ancient confessions. "One Lord, one faith, one baptism. . . ." (Ephesians 4:4.) This experienced ecumenism of the church in time is a fact with wide-ranging implications, even though these implications are more often ignored than recalled.

But there is a second, less obvious, significance in the phrase, ecumenism in time. For the life of the church can be visualized as providing the brackets within which its own time is located, this time being a mode of measuring distances between what has already come and what has not yet come. In every period of chronological time, the church lives in the present. This historical present of the church is decisively different from the historical present of the world, just as the memory and hope of the church are decisively different. The historical present of the church is defined by the peculiar triangle of forces which faith recognizes as operating within its life in each today. This triangle may be described as created by three interlocking lines of divine activity: what God has done in heaven, what he has done already on earth, what he is about to do on earth. In terms of the church's response these three lines can be indicated by the three terms: revelation, memory, hope. These three lines determine the historical present of the church, dictate the time of its life, and establish a structural similarity between the situation of the church in the twentieth century and the situation in the other centuries. Ecumenism in time points to the fact that all churches, of whatever century, live in a historical present which is defined by the revelation of God's activity in heaven, by the memory of what he has done in our midst, and by the expectation of what he is about to complete in our midst.

This line of thought is difficult to chart, but the difficulty stems more from our habitual patterns of thought than from our actual experience within the church. We have already suggested different elements in this experience which provide boundaries to each historical present, to each "now" in the church's life. For example, in Chapter I, we have described how the New Testament church understood itself by relation to God's glory. Those who have been glorified (Romans 8:30) are enabled by the Spirit of glory to do everything "to the glory of God." (1 Corinthians 10:31.) The singing of the doxology indicates that the time of their life reaches backward to events when God has revealed his glory and reaches ahead to the full consummation of this "glorious circle." "When Christ who is our life appears, then you also will appear with him in glory." (Colossians 3:4.) So, too, when the church is experiencing the powerful attack from God's adversary, Satan, it measures the inception and termination of this earthly struggle by the revelation of the victory already won in heaven. It understands this struggle in terms of an immediate past and an immediate future when, as repercussions of this heavenly struggle, earthly events disclose God's power through the cross, first to challenge and to enrage, and then to overcome and to enslave the demonic militia.[2] When we shift to a different New Testament idiom, to its understanding of the church as the holy city, a similar pattern emerges. The historical present is a pilgrim trek bounded simultaneously by the Jerusalem which is above and the Jerusalem which is to come. Ecumenical solidarity stems from the fact that all the pilgrims (in their varying congregations) are embarked on a voyage which begins and ends in the same city.[3]

The historical present of the Church has dimensions, therefore, which make it unique. On the one hand, in this *now* the communion of saints participates already in eternal life. On the other hand, this very participation involves it in earthly tasks wherein it stands on the battle line between God and the devil, between *gloria dei* and *gloria mundi*, between Jerusalem and Babylon. It now uses time to measure the distances appropriate to these tasks, tasks which inherently bear the personal imprint of a Lord who himself has bridged the distance between heaven and earth, the coming age and the old age.

It was inevitable, therefore, that the apostles, in recognizing the newness of this situation, should use diverse ways in picturing its newness. Their unique stance modified their comprehension of both time and eternity. No longer could they visualize eternity as the time line extended infinitely into the future, nor as a static realm remote from the times of creaturely existence. They could not visualize the calendar as the dictator of human destinies. The routines of the calendar now were invested potentially with an eternal weight of glory. In coming near to men, the kingdom had marked the fulness of time. In the pres-

---

[2] cf. Chapter II.
[3] cf. Chapter III.

ent moment of decision, therefore, men stand between what God has done and what he has begun to do. They stand within the brackets of the kingdom's coming. And this parenthesis is not a period when movement ceases, but a period when the new age moves toward men, from Christ's faithfulness toward man's faith, and from Christ's life toward man's life.

Accurate description of this time-between, therefore, becomes a matter of strategic importance for both historical and theological studies. Almost all contemporary schools of research admit the eschatological character of the New Testament community. But this fact is variously construed. In futurist eschatology, the kingdom is considered to be wholly future yet imminent. The interim which controls present action is judged to be the temporal distance between the present moment on the earthly time line and the future moment on the same time line when the advent of the kingdom is anticipated. The shorter this distance is, the more critical and decisive becomes the action. Both Jesus and Paul calculated a very short time span, and, according to this view, both were mistaken.

In realized eschatology, on the other hand, the kingdom is viewed as having come already in a historical event, whether at the outset of Jesus' ministry, at his death-resurrection, or at Pentecost. The obedience of faith is therefore a present response to this past event and is no longer necessarily oriented toward Christ's future advent. The time span between the present moment and the promised consummation has lost its power to change today's decisions. Nothing can happen in the future which will vitally alter the present situation. Since eternal life in Christ is now an open option, the only question is whether by faith and obedience we choose to appropriate the life "that is hid with Christ in God."

A third alternative is to free the existential moment of faith from any kind of *temporal* dependence upon either the first or the second comings of Christ. *Temporal* duration is a trap which enslaves the human spirit; only the Word of God, welcomed by the decision of faith, can free men from the lock step of time. Only in this present moment can a person achieve authentic existence through the grace of God in Christ. The time which separates this present moment from either end of the interim must be telescoped into the absolute demand to die now with Christ, into the absolute gift of living now with him. By faith in Christ man dies to every bondage (the self, the world, sin, time, death); then the living Christ raises the dead self to freedom, to an absolute openness toward the future, to a hope which does not depend on earthly circumstance. What is now important is *not* the chronological distance from either an ancient or a future event, but subjective distance between despair and faith in the redemption of man.

Few scholars, however, are wholly content with any of these three positions: with futurist eschatology, realized eschatology, or a fully existentialized eschatology. Yet all three have genuine merit, both historically and theologically. If we are to make progress in recovering the New Testament pattern of thought, we must do justice to the evidence for all three, and at the same time we must devise a more adequate way of describing the historical present—its beginning, its end, and the forms in which eternal life supports the church between the beginning and the end.

## THE TIME OF THE CHURCH'S PRAYER

It is at this point that I believe we can receive unexpected help from the familiar *Lord's Prayer*. This prayer, as we have seen, defines the interim in terms of the time between what has happened *in heaven* and what is about to happen *on earth*. This suggests a perspective within which all three "eschatologies" have a place. Here, for example, we have the explicit conviction that the relationship of the community to the kingdom is that of *prayer*. Nothing is more highly existential than this. Prayer is genuine only to the degree that the present moment holds a genuine eschatological urgency, an absolute decisiveness. In this Lord's Prayer, when the words perfectly correspond to the heart's intent, the holiness of God's name confronts the sin of man, and the bondage of sin yields to the plea for forgiveness. The power of God's kingdom comes to free man's spirit from anxiety and trial, and this power is embodied in the beggar's cry for bread and for deliverance from evil.

There are, of course, other aspects of this Prayer which do not yield easily to an interpretation along purely existentialist lines. This, for instance, is a prayer of the family of God, a prayer in which the family expresses its total dependence for everything it needs on the Father. An individualistic existentialism will hardly do justice to this corporate act. Again, the prayer emerges from a historical situation in which something decisive has already happened in heaven, although its repercussions have not yet fully transpired on earth. The community stands praying in the midst of this event, where God's active purpose is operative. It stands between the revealed and announced Word of God and the events through which that Word returns to God with its mission accomplished. The community stands in the midst of this creative and redemptive action of God, linked by its prayer both to the action, as it becomes effective, and to the reaction, as it moves toward completion. Here, then, in the moment of prayer, the glory of God produces man's freedom. This is a thoroughly existential event. But the boundaries of the event reach beyond the event, for those who pray recognize their *now* as a time set between the times. Because this interval reaches from heavenly event to earthly event, those who pray are not, of course, prompted to measure it in months and years. But they find it equally impossible completely to sunder communal memory and hope from earthly time, because the events themselves are in truth temporal as well as eternal— the life of heaven encompasses the life of a visible community and is embodied within it. Members of the Church, therefore, do not ask to be taken from earth to heaven, nor for a hypothetical kingdom to be realized on earth, nor for a kingdom already established in time to become world-wide; they beg that a kingdom which has been realized in heaven may come on earth.

Insofar as the prayer springs from the recognition of what God has already done, it reflects realized eschatology. " 'The law and the prophets were until John; since then the good news of the kingdom of God is preached.' " (Luke 16:16.) If the prayer was first used during the ministry of Jesus, it presupposed his prophetic proclamation that God had begun his warfare against Satan with the expulsion of Satan from heaven. When it was used by the church after the climactic events of the Passion, it presupposed the apostolic proclamation that God had disclosed his heavenly power by exalting "this Jesus whom you crucified." The petition "Thy will be done on earth" was inseparable from the affirmation "as it now has been done in heaven," and this affirmation embraced all that God had done in breaking the bonds of death and in exalting Jesus' brothers to "sit with him in heavenly places." It embraced whatever miracles had been wrought among men by the Holy Spirit. Each celebration of baptism and the Eucharist was nothing less than the celebration of an emancipation which had been accomplished in heaven and which was even now being extended to earth. Vast treasures "laid up in heaven" were even now being mediated to the church, the value of which was indicated in such terms as joy, peace, forgiveness, mercy, hope, and the inheritance. From heaven came the daily manna. In heaven the saints had their names written, their home city, their white robes, and their powerful advocate. All this, and more too, gave expression to the fact that in heaven is their living Lord and that they already form a community of the first-born (Luke 12: 33; Mark 11:30; 15:7; 19:38; John 6:31; 2 Corinthians 5:1, 2; Colossians 4:1; Philippians 3:20; Hebrews 12:23; 1 Peter 1:4).

In these varied ways, the historical present of the Church was defined by a temporal boundary, by what had already happened in the reclamation of earthly territory by its rightful King. Yet the New Testament church did not, and could not, calculate the distance between this present and this past by reference to calendar years alone. It did not do this, because the inner meaning of the present decisions of faith did not depend upon whether it had been five or fifty years since Calvary. It could not do this because the events which marked the coming of the new age, from its inception onward, could not be confined to moments of earthly time. Who could be so audacious as to date an act of God, especially when this action was so freighted with final judgment and redemption? On the other hand, the apostles did not eliminate temporal distance entirely from their understanding of the church's life. God's kingdom has been manifested on earth. The harvesting has begun. Of that harvest the existence of the praying family is the first fruit.

Therefore this family also recognizes a future boundary to its present life. It expects the full harvest. It begs with eschatological passion: "Thy kingdom come." The new age which comes from heaven always comes from God's future into the community's present. Knowing what God has done, it knows, although this knowledge does not rule out surprise, what God is about to do. This is why in its life on earth infinite confidence elicits infinite risk, radical peace prompts radical participation in the agony of creation, the joy of its Lord impels participation in his sufferings. The community which understands the phrase "as it is in heaven" to include its own actual participation in eternal life also finds maximum pertinence in the petition: "Deliver us from the evil one."

## The Time of the Church's Suffering

This leads us to a second way in which early Christian prophets visualized the historical present: as the period between the initiation and the culmination of a cosmic war. The prophets understood this interval as determined by the inner logic of redemptive suffering. Moreover, they understood that such heavenly victory as had been won by the Messiah could be extended to earth only through a church which would embody his form, i.e., the form of a Servant. What, then, is the vantage point from which the prophets described the time between the times? Their stance was that of earthly weakness and defeat, of fighting battles in which, like that fought in Gethsemane, heavenly triumph is masked by earthly failure. For the fullest exposition of this prophetic paradigm we may turn to the Revelation to John.

Along with other New Testament writers, the prophet John believed that with the fall of Satan from heaven, the battle had become climactic on earth and would continue until the last trumpet sounds. He therefore describes, in a kaleidoscope of shifting scenes, the time before this trumpet. For the first of these scenes we look at chapters 12 and 13. Here he proclaims that Satan's fall from heaven occurs simultaneously with two connected earthly events: the slaying of the Lamb by the dragon and the courage by which men conquer the same dragon by "the blood of the Lamb and by the word of their testimony." (12:11.) God's truth is the direct opposite of men's illusion. The conflict between truth and lie therefore produces paradoxes; consequently, the prophet must utilize these paradoxes to help the church discern the truth. The Lamb was slain, but his wound accomplished the healing of the nations. The beast was also wounded unto death by the Lamb, but in the eyes of the world its mortal wound had been healed. (13:3.) Ever and again the omnipotence of the beast appeared to be vindicated in his triumph over the Lamb and his followers. "Who is like the beast? Who can fight against it?" (13:4.) God allowed it to make war on the saints and to conquer them. Yes, but in that conquest, the beast actually demonstrated his impotence, while the saints actually manifested, by their acceptance of death, the glorious power of the Lamb. Thus the prophet disclosed the continuing situation of the church—always militant, yet always triumphant so long as its militancy accords with the meekness of the Lamb.[4]

In this situation how did the prophet indicate the temporal duration of the warfare? At first sight the answer is precise: the present period will last for "a time and times and half a time" (12:14) or the 3½ years of apocalyptic tradition. What happens during these years? Pursuit and protection. From the

---

[4]cf. author's essay in *Journal of Biblical Literature,* 1953, pp. 93-101.

moment of his defeat in heaven the dragon pursues the messianic community, but God protects "the woman" until her mission is accomplished. Pursued for "a time and times and half a time," she is protected and nourished in the wilderness. (12: 14.) Protection in persecution is her allotted portion during this present interval. (12:6.)

Another measurement of the war's duration appears in Chapter 11, in connection with the story of the temple and two lampstands. Here the prophet sees the nations trampling over the holy city for 42 months, but they are unable to destroy "the temple of God and the altar and those who worship there." (11:1-3.) Again appears this double motif of pursuit and protection. In the temple are two lampstands, identified as two witnesses who have been given power to prophesy. They exercise this power for a period of 1,260 days (which equals the 42 months and the 3½ years). Throughout this period the Devil buffets them, but they, too, like the woman and like the temple, are protected until they have finished their testimony. Prophesying in sackcloth, their *work* is invulnerable; but *they* are not. For when their prophecy has been given, the beast is permitted to kill them. (11:7.) The place of their death is carefully identified: it is Jerusalem, Sodom and Egypt, the very same city "where their Lord was crucified." Like his death, theirs seems to the demon-deceived world to be proof of their failure. (11: 10.) But their resurrection, like his, discloses their victory and the glory of the God of heaven. In this context the interval of 42 months has a specific symbolic value. It measures the distance between his death and theirs, or between his resurrection and theirs, or between the inception of their mission and its completion. During this period their message is immune to the devil's attacks; but the messengers themselves are vulnerable. In fact, the period ends when protection is withdrawn from the messengers, and they vindicate their victory by sharing the utter weakness and forsakenness of their Master.

Still another version of the same temporal span is sketched by the versatile pen of the prophet in Chapter 17. Here the love of the Lamb for Jerusalem, his Bride, is set over against the fickle passion which the devil shows for Babylon, the mother and home of harlots. Babylon has now its period of flourishing, when the harlot gets drunk with the blood of the saints. During this same period the love of the Lamb for his city remains quite hidden. But the time draws near when the implicit enmity between the beast and the harlot will be openly displayed. This moment will simultaneously display the love of the Lamb for his Bride. Until this disclosure, only the faithful witness knows that Christ is already sovereign over the nations as one "who was and is and is to come." He therefore knows that the sovereignty of the beast is illusory: he is one "who was and *is not* and is to ascend." This ascension of the devil from the bottomless pit corresponds to the final forsakenness of the church when it joins in the Lord's dereliction. But the devil is released from the abyss only in order to be consigned to perdition. In his coming he will demonstrate the truth that he "is not." By the sharpest contrast, the Lamb's victory will demonstrate the truth that he "is," and that he is the only true Alpha and Omega.

This same logic, I believe, lies behind the picture of the millennium in Chapter 20. Here the devil, first cast from heaven, is then caught and cast into the abyss where he is bound for 1,000 years. During this period, he "is not"; that is, he has no power to frustrate the message and mission of the church. God does, in fact, protect his people. The word and work of the martyrs are alive with power. They reign on thrones. But before their triumph can be fully disclosed to all earth dwellers, Satan must be loosed from the pit. Before the powers of the new age can overcome Death itself, the devil must be allowed to unleash all his forces, including Death and Hades. The church must accept its total vulnerability to the power of these enemies. Only then can the new heaven and the new earth and the holy city be established in all their glory, in such fulness as to include "the kings of the earth." (21:24.) In this picture as in the others, the historical present is understood as a time of protection and a time of persecution. This time will come to

an end in the removal of protection and the climactic demonstration of the full power of the Devil, Death, and Hell. But
this "end" will but vindicate the paradigmatic truth of the Passion story, when the story of Jesus en route to Jerusalem becomes the story of his people en route to the same holy city.
En route his church views its present as the same ordained for
bearing his cross, knowing that his cross is the continuing channel of redemption as God's city descends from heaven to earth.
The struggle with Satan is a necessary feature in this descent.
The struggle remains until the church has shared fully in drink-
ing the cup of its Lord. But the gathering momentum of the
struggle can be met with peace and joy, because this very momentum is a sign of redemption drawing near. (Luke 21:20-28.)

It is quite possible, of course, that the pictures of the church's
suffering which fill the Book of Revelation are not typical of the
whole New Testament. Yet when we read the Synoptic Gospels, a similar pattern of thought emerges. Consider the story
in Luke of Jesus' initial work in Nazareth. (6:16-30.) His
message enrages his listeners, who try to throw him over a
cliff; but God protects him from harm. The Messiah is both
pursued and protected until at Golgotha the enemy is allowed
free play for his designs. (23:18-43.) When Jesus sets his face
to go to Jerusalem, he knows what will happen there at his
"exodus," but he knows that during the interim he is immune
to the plots of Herod, "for it cannot be that a prophet should
perish away from Jerusalem." (13:31-35.) It is entirely fitting
therefore that when Jesus dispatches his disciples on their mission, he should assure them both of the success of their mission
and of the termination of that mission by the hostility of the
devil.

A recent perceptive study of the Gospel of Mark provides
ample documentation for that Gospel. Mark sees "Jesus and the
church engaged in the same cosmic struggle against the same
demonic force of evil." "The experiences of the church are
presented in the Marcan apocalypse as prophesied by and mod-
elled after the history of Jesus." "Mark's understanding of the

church is rooted in a new understanding of history as the interplay of blessedness and suffering." Mark views the time of salvation "in terms of the struggle with which it begins and the final victory with which it terminates."[5]

Against the mythological background of cosmic struggle, then, the New Testament witnesses to the present time of the church's life as a time of salvation, in which the gift of heavenly life precipitates an earthly struggle wherein God first protects and then abandons his messengers, and thus enables them to share fully in the victory of his Messiah. This present time has boundaries, it has a redemptive past and a redemptive future, but the character of these boundaries defies all efforts at measurement in terms of the solar calendar.

## THE TIME OF THE CHURCH'S MISSION

I move all too hastily to a brief consideration of a third mode of thought by which the early Church articulated its understanding of its historical present. Here I shift to the vocabulary and idiom of the Fourth Gospel, where the phrase the kingdom of God is replaced usually by the term *life,* sometimes characterized as aeonic or eternal life. Strikingly absent is the drama of apocalyptic warfare, although the figure of the devil remains a major actor. As preparation for interpreting this new idiom, let us recall a view which was mentioned in our discussion of the city where God dwells, the new Jerusalem.

This city is both the source and the goal of the church's existence. Jerusalem is both our mother and our future residence. We have come to this city—and it will come to us. We are its citizens, and therefore we move in pilgrimage toward its walls. A similar pattern appears in the Synoptics, Hebrews, and Paul. Jesus' disciples are sons of the kingdom and as sons they seek to enter it. A person is a son of him from whom he comes and toward whom he goes. Sons of God are heirs of God. This inheritance has a double reference: they are born of the prom-

[5]James M. Robinson, *The Problem of History in Mark,* S.C.M. Press, London, U. S. Distributor Allenson, Naperville, Illinois. Used by permission.

ise and of the Spirit; and they move toward the fulness of the promise, toward the mature man, the one new man who is Christ. Implicit within this mode of thought is a profound eschatology, a subtle far-reaching ecclesiology, and an existential appraisal of the mysterious in-between period in which the church stands. The church comes from God and goes to God. This is the basic truth. Her life spans the time from the coming to the going, supported by the assurance that "he who began a good work in you will bring it to completion." (Phil. 1:6.)

In the Fourth Gospel the mystery of the Son of man is frequently expressed as the mystery of his coming and his going. He comes from God. He is sent from God to do God's work. His authority, his power, his love, his truth—all these are marks of his place of origin. His miracles are signs that he is from above; more than this, they are works done by the Father. The food which he offers is heavenly manna.

> "For the bread of God is that which *comes down* from heaven, and gives life to the world." They said to him, "Lord, give us this bread always."
> Jesus said to them, "I am the bread of life; he who comes to me shall not hunger, and he who believes in me shall never thirst. . . . For I have *come down* from heaven, not to do my own will, but the will of him who sent me. . . ." (John 6:33-35, 38.)

Such a descent requires, for completion, a corresponding ascent. The whence of his life determines the whither. "No one has ascended into heaven but he who descended from heaven, the Son of man.'" (1:13.) He is "the Way" because in his ministry the whence and the whither are revealed. Those who recognize the one recognize the other. His work is in large part to mediate this understanding of his from-ness and his towardness. He comes—he abides—he goes—this is the simple sequence, closely interrelated. And the evangelist leaves no doubt about Jesus' origin or destiny, even though none of the participants in the story (other than Jesus and perhaps the devil) discerned the full truth. "Thomas said to him, 'Lord we do not know where you are going; how can we know the way?'" (14:5.) Jesus ascends above, he goes to heaven, he returns to his Father. None of these phrases can be rightly interpreted if in our minds the geographical denotation is primary. John is not interested in celestial maps. He is dealing with the cosmic scope of Jesus and his work on earth. To him, the only alternative to coming from God is not a neutral status of simple earthly origin but coming from the devil.

> He said to them, "You are from below, I am from above; you are of this world, I am not of this world. . . .
> "You are of your father the devil, and your will is to do your father's desires." (8:23, 44.)

Human wills, embodied in earthly actions, emerge from and point toward some heavenly paternity. Thus the Fourth Gospel defines the whole work of Jesus as the interim between his descent and his ascent. And everything he says and does derives its meaning from both his coming and his going. Apart from either, his claim on men would be canceled.

A saving knowledge of the Son of man, therefore, requires the recognition of his whence and whither. "I know whence I have come and whither I am going, but you do not know whence I come or whither I am going." (8:14.) This recognition is not easily accomplished. In fact, to recognize Jesus' origin and destiny requires that a person himself shares the same heavenly origin and destiny. This is what is signified by being born again, or by being born from above. Note three ways of describing this birth:

> "Unless one is born anew, he cannot see the kingdom of God." (3:3.)
> "Unless one is born of water and the Spirit, he cannot enter the kingdom." (3:5.)
> "The wind blows where it wills, and you hear the sound of it, but you do not know whence it comes or whither it

goes; so it is with every one who is born of the Spirit."
3:8.)

Children of God are born of God. (1:13.) It is assumed that
those who are thus born bear witness to what they have seen
of heavenly actualities. (3:11.) Their deeds are "wrought in
God." (3:21.) To believe in the Son is to believe in the Father
who sent the Son and this is to pass from death to life. (5:24.)
This transition is a signal that the Father has given the reborn
man to the Son. (6:37.) Faith in Christ means that the new
son shares in the same origin as the only begotten Son. And
therefore they share alike in the mission of being sent into the
world. They have been given to Jesus by the Father, and Jesus
gives them eternal life.

But this new sending includes necessarily a new *whither* as
well as a new *whence*. This *whither* in Jesus' case is capable of
various true descriptions. He is going to Jerusalem. He is going to wash their feet, to give his life for his sheep, to be lifted
up in judgment of the world. In all these ways he completes
his mission. And by fulfilling his mission he goes to his Father
who sent him. The *whither* of his disciples corresponds: they
are called to hate their life, to wash one another's feet, to follow
Jesus, and to feed his sheep. It is along such a path that they
complete the task on which he sends them. It is clear, poign-
antly clear, that the disciples did not, during pre-Golgotha days,
understand either his whither or theirs. "Where I am going you
cannot follow me now." To them the trip to Jerusalem on which
they accompanied him was not their return to the Father. Yet
behind their trip lay the promise "You shall follow afterward."
(13:36.)

Their ignorance of the Way explains why the Gospel of
John places great stress on the visit of the risen Lord to his
disciples. This visit marks their own discovery of the Way, the
whence, the whither. Now they can be truly sent. Now the
Spirit comes to them. Their belief now actually brings light.
Henceforth they know whence they have come and whither they

go. Jesus comes to them and breathes the Spirit on them. And among the most pregnant words in all the records of such events is this:

"I am ascending to my Father and your Father, to my God and your God." (20:17.)

This defines the common *whither*. Now the *whence* of the disciples is made inseparable from their *whither*. The span of their ministry is given a beginning and an end which corresponds to those of the Son of man. His time is not their time, but they have a time—a time determined by their sending, their mission, their destiny. And their time is a time during which God the Father and Christ the Son abide with them. For them, at last, the Way is understood to be the Life.

The evangelist explicitly includes within this same Way the whole body of disciples, not only the original twelve but also all who "are to believe . . . through their word." (17:20.) There is and can be but one sending, one gift of glory, one knowledge, and one love. (17:21-26.) Eternal life is shared within the world. "I do not pray that thou shouldst take them out of the world." (17:15.) The church does not go to heaven to find a home with the Father and the Son. Rather they come to make their home with the church in the world. (14:23.) Here is the residence of the Spirit and the eschatological peace. (14:26, 27; 20:21-22.) The time in which the church lives as church must be sharply distinguished from the time of the world's existence for the simple reason that the church is not "of the world." Its *whence* and *whither* are its very life, eternal life. This is why the world hates the church as it hated him who is the resurrection and the life.

We have now expounded three different idioms used in the New Testament to express the church's understanding of its historical present as a time of salvation, of heavenly life: the idiom of the Lord's Prayer, of the messianic woes, and of the whence-and-whither. There are vast differences in nuances among these three. Nothing is gained by ignoring this diversity.

The diversity may be traced to separate linguistic ancestries. The idiom of the Lord's Prayer may be most similar to the language and outlook of the Pharisees and the Essenes. Multiple parallels may be discerned in the literature of the Rabbis and of the Qumran sectaries. The idiom of the Book of Revelation is a legacy of the apocalyptic mind, with parallels in the pseud-epigraphic literature. The idiom of descent and ascent in the Fourth Gospel reflects the outlook of Gnosticism, both Jewish and Christian, with parallels in the writings of that amorphous movement. The divergence in ancestries, however, did not prevent early Christians from converting all the idioms and patterns of thought into their own unique understanding of their own situation.

In all three, the axiomatic conviction is that the church has its being in relationship to the God from whom and to whom are all things. All assume as real a temporal interim between the *from* and the *to*. All accent the nearness of heaven to earth —not as a spatial element in the cosmos—but as the source of the double-leveled conflict: the hostility between church and world, which corresponds to the conflict in heaven between God and Satan. All subordinate the durational element in this interim to the mission of the church to the world. None visualizes God as enslaved by the temporal measurements of the world. His redemptive purposes embrace and set bounds to the times of his creation. He sends his people into the world and dwells with them there. And he conveys to them there something which the world can neither give nor destroy: a knowledge of origin and destiny which is creative of and definitive of their life. Their memory is a memory of what God has done: his calling and sending, his creation of them as sons by new birth from above, his gift of the Holy Spirit, events which point back to heavenly origin. Their hope is already laid up for them in heaven, but they move toward it as an inheritance for sons, as a peace for the sons of peace. Memory is not of an event which rapidly recedes into the dimness of the past. Nor does hope anticipate a consummation which is progressively postponed as the years fly

by. Impersonal views of time have not subjugated memory and
hope. No, memory and hope retain their power over the living
present. In each case the memory of heavenly deed elicits a
sure hope of earthly consequence. In one sense, both memory
and hope are the "projections" of a praying, suffering, witnessing, and tempted church. But these projections are as true or
as false as the revelation to the church that its very life is first
of all a projection on earth of God's saving presence in Jesus
Christ. This, to be sure, is what the church believes most firmly
about Christ—his life is a projection on earth of heavenly power
and glory. More than this, his ministry serves as a paradigm, a
model, of the church's ministry. The interim of his story, from
the whence to the whither, becomes the essential clue to the
interim of the church's story. It is this horizon which makes
the church an eschatological community, the realm of eternal
life. This horizon comes clearly into view in the confession from
the Anaphora of St. John Chrysostom: "Thou didst not cease to
do all things until thou hadst brought us back to heaven, and
hadst endowed us with the kingdom which is to come."[6]

The life of the church, therefore, is inseparable from the environment provided by God's glory, the new Jerusalem, and the
new age. This environment produces, at least in the New Testament writers, a unique awareness of the historical present. It
produces also a unique set of answers to the question: where
lie the boundaries of this community? In doxological terms
these boundaries follow the line between the glory of God and
the glory of the world. In mythological terms, they follow the
line between the army of God and the army of Satan. In typological terms, the line between Jerusalem and Babylon. All
these motifs underscore the truths that God alone, through his
activity among and through men, determines the boundary between the kingdom of his Son—with its dying life, its joyful affliction, its offensive wisdom—and the kingdom of darkness which
is pervaded, let us not forget, by religious convictions that

---

[6] I am indebted for this citation to Father Alexander Schmemann.

eternal life is something very different from that life which invaded the kingdoms of the world through the victory of the cross.

To those who seek a viable definition of the church, a systematic and normative doctrine which would do service in either theological or ecclesiastical wars, the New Testament imagery must seem very frustrating. The very nature of these idioms makes a set of precise conclusions impossible. But even though such a study leads us farther and farther from the goal of an accurate and exact doctrine, this in itself may yield greater comprehension of the magnitude of the Christian community. The reality may be of such a nature that the more we understand it, the less we are able to draw its boundaries and map its terrain. Does this mean, then, that the effort to relate the Una Sancta to the church in Grover's Corners must be given up as an impossible task? Must we forsake the empirical church for the heavenly church? Not at all. For all of the New Testament efforts to describe the scope and scale of the church's life presuppose one thing. They presuppose that we are in close and intimate communion with a congregation. It is life together which enables us to comprehend the glory of God. And this life together is possible only in some town, whether it be Grover's Corners or Grundy Center.

Chapter V

# THE SCOPE OF
# CHRIST'S WORK

The one Church of Christ . . . is the sphere of action of the heavenly Christ, all its members being in Christ and belonging together to a supranatural kinship. All the gifts they possess and all the activity they display are a continuation of the work of Christ, who is the One who is originating and co-ordinating this whole in order to realize the one final result, that will become manifest in the eschatological future as the one People of God.[1]

—JOHANNES DE ZWAAN

---

[1]Johannes de Zwaan, in *Aux Sources de la Tradition Chretienne*, Melanges offerts a Maurice Coguel, Neuchatel: Delachaux et Niestle, p. 270. Used by permission.

Several observations may now be made concerning the import of previous chapters. They accent basic New Testament convictions that Christian community is not so much an institutional as a supranatural entity, which in magnitude incorporates both earthly and heavenly activities. This magnitude has dimensions of height and depth which are incontestibly actual yet which are nevertheless intangible. Such boundaries as we have sketched cannot be reduced to space and time by the instruments of a terrestrial surveyor. In consequence, the effort to apprehend and to describe those boundaries may draw us farther and farther away from the personal situation of the individual member. Engaged in charting horizons, we readily lose the sharp sense of living and working at a specific point within those horizons. The element of concreteness easily evaporates. And so the gulf widens between *that* church "out there" or "back there" and *this* community in which I now hold a more or less temporary membership. It is with this gulf that this concluding chapter deals. Let us begin, then, with appraisals of the extent of this gulf.

## CHRIST'S CHURCH

First of all, the statement of J. de Zwaan, cited on the preceding page, elicits a comment or two. In his statements, Professor de Zwaan attempted to summarize the results of his exploration of the church idea in the New Testament. Applying rigorously the methods of historical and linguistic scholarship—and there are few to contest his greatness as a scholar—he arrived at the conclusion that early Christians viewed the church primarily as "the sphere of action of the Heavenly Christ." Before they thought *church* they had already thought *Christ*.[2] His picture moved through their minds before their lips could form the word for church. If they visualized the community as Israel, as kingdom, as the people, or as the city, they first had in Christ recognized the King of this society. The image of the community as a flock presupposed him as both Shepherd and Lamb. The image of the branches made sense only as part of the image of the vine. The conception of family was corollary to the conception of the Son and elder brother. The body was governed by the Head, the temple by the high priest or the cornerstone, the bride by the bridegroom. Behind each figurative expression for the church there appears the figure of its Lord.[3] To repeat, saying "church" meant that one had first said "Christ."

How different the practice in modern America! What thought customarily crosses our minds before we say "church"? Different people will, of course have different answers, and sometimes the same person will give a different answer on different occasions. Often the first picture on the mind's screen will be that of a familiar building located at a familiar spot. We think of the church in close association with the post office or the public school. Again, we may associate the word almost exclusively with one hour in the week: eleven o'clock on Sunday morning. This is when the church comes alive, when we go to church. Sometimes the picture which flashes across our mind before we

[2]Zwaan, *op. cit.*
[3]cf. *Jesus and His People*, Paul Minear, New York, 1956.

say "church" is a certain pastor or priest in whose presence we are conscious of the existence of the church. At other times, we visualize a particular gathering of men and women, who meet periodically in social affairs, to transact the organization's business, and to govern certain educational and benevolent enterprises. In making out the annual income tax report, people are accustomed to associate church with Community Fund, Boy Scouts, and the Red Cross. On many lips the term "church" is strangely incomplete unless it is accompanied by an adjective. That is, before we say the noun, we have thought Methodist or Baptist or Lutheran. And it may be true that for us the adjective is more effective than the noun in defining what we have in mind. If so, the noun and adjective may refer to a particular parish, sharply distinguished from neighboring parishes even where the same adjective appears, as, for example, "The Presbyterian Church"; or we may have quite a different object in mind: a national or an international body, with its officials and boards, its organization and budget. The Protestant mind almost instinctively excludes Catholic and Orthodox communions from consideration, while the Catholic mind returns the compliment. Yes, the adjective can be more decisive than the noun. In some minds, the word "church," before it is uttered, already implies a particular strand in cultural and national history, and therefore connotes a movement through the centuries which has helped to shape the laws and habits, the coloration and configuration, of American life. So we could continue the list of mental associations which give to the spoken syllable its initial cargo of meaning. But our intention here is not so much to demonstrate the weasel properties of this simple word as to illustrate the fact that in most contemporary contexts we do not first think "Christ" before we say "church."

There is another habit of speech which registers the gulf between New Testament times and our own. This habit of speech is subtly hidden behind the pronouns customarily used. Whether we have in our minds our congregation or our denomination, we most naturally point to this entity by saying "it" or "they." Occasionally, to be sure, in an imaginary dialogue with this entity (or in direct address to its leader or its representatives) we may say "you." But rarely in our thinking about the church do we spontaneously say "we." And perhaps even more rarely would we find it natural to say of this community "he" (referring to the Lord whose "body" this is) or "she" (referring to his "Bride" or his "mother").

Just this habit in thinking bespeaks a definite orientation toward this community. By thinking "it," we normally acknowledge not only its impersonal, collective character, but also the existence of an actual though nebulous distance between ourselves and this object of speech. "It" is something about which I think and speak objectively. At the moment of thought I am separate. Even if I have joined "it," it remains over against me as a distinct reality. Its distance from me is reflected in my questions: Shall I attend it regularly? How much money and time shall I devote to it? Do I enjoy it? Is it doing a good job? Why doesn't it do it better? What, after all, do I think of it? In giving this form to these questions I assume that I am standing outside this particular community rather than within it. And I am loath to relinquish this seat as a judge before whom the church must appear, and that almost daily, for my verdict. No matter how fully I have been drawn into the program of this my church, it remains quite noticeably distant from my innermost selfhood. Only seldom is the *it* of distance-thinking replaced instinctively by the *we* of solidarity-thinking.

It was far more usual and natural for early Christians to use the first-person-corporate in speaking of the church; it was in fact not only unnatural, but recognized as disloyal, to view oneself as an individual apart from the fellowship. To the extent that Jesus Christ, in his living and ruling power, constituted the innermost center and the outermost horizons of the community, to that same extent he constituted the new being of every member, and the horizons of that member's existence. For where center and circumference of two circles are identical, the areas of the two circles coincide. Those within the circle are united,

whatever their private stories might contain, by the same boundaries of death and life. And these very boundaries are not only
exterior and remote but also interior and near, as near as finger
to hand. For what surrounds the death and life of this community and each of its members is not an "It" but a "Thou."
He lives at both circumference and center, beginning and end.
Before saying church, think Christ.

When the relationship between Christ and church is made
primary, the shape of our questions concerning individual relationships to the church is transformed. Instead of venturing
my judgment concerning the church, I listen rather to what the
church asks of me. What does the church believe about me?
To what degree does it trust me? What can it accomplish
through me? What is its view of the significance and purpose
of my work? Within the horizons of its mission where does my
vocation fit? Perhaps *it* is the judge before whom I stand.
Perhaps it has a truer understanding of my role than I have of
its role.

## BELONGING TO THE CHURCH

Let us consider, for example, two opposite ways of interpreting the sentence: "I belong to the church." What does this
word *belong* signify? America is notorious as a nation of joiners.
Once an American has joined any organization, he belongs to it,
whether it is a hiking club, a college fraternity, or the P.T.A.
If a person has joined the First Congregational Church, he belongs to that congregation. He increases its roster by one; it increases the number of his organizational commitments by one.
Perhaps no greater or deeper change than this is recorded in the
life of either congregation or member. To be sure, if a person
is listed in *Who's Who*, he will include in his list of member-
ships only the more impressive organizations to which he belongs. They not only help to identify him but also add to his
prestige. And if a congregation has some members who are on
their own accounts notable figures, their membership adds to its
prestige. But in the wide segments of our culture the distinc-

tion between a church member and a nonchurch member is much less significant than the distinction between members of one Christian group and another. In short, it is not so significant to belong to a church as to belong to a specific church. Only perhaps in the case of the Communist party is there a radically different implication. The party is the thing, not the cell. Membership signifies more than a voluntary act of partial commitment by an individual. In this case, one signifies that he is accepting status as a tool in the hands of the party. One becomes a soldier under orders, and these are the orders of an international agency. It is assumed that henceforth he is committed wholly to the interests of the party, and that whatever significance his life may have will be conferred on him by the party.

How strikingly different was the conception of belonging in the New Testament! There is actually no comparable word in New Testament Greek. Where the Revised Standard Version has adopted the English word "belong," it is by way of a free translation of a prepositional phrase or the possessive case. The phrase "belong to the *church*" is amazingly rare even in the English translations. (Acts 9:2; 12:1.) The dominant note is rather to belong to Christ or to God. And here the English almost always is a rendering of the possessive genitive. Paul belongs to God (Acts 27:23) because he is his; the Roman, Corinthian, and Galatian Christians belong to Christ because they are his. (Romans 8:9; 1 Corinthians 15:23; Galatians 5:24.) As a slave belongs to its owner or as a son belongs to his parents, so the believer belongs to Christ. Belonging is something initiated by the one who has called, claimed, and bought a slave. Between those who belong to the world (Colossians 2:20; John 3:31) and those who belong to Christ lies the death and resurrection of both Lord and servants. (Romans 7:4; 8:9; Galatians 5:24.) In this transition *day* has dawned, and sons of the day belong to it. (1 Thessolonians 5:8.) Only as one first belongs to Christ can he rightly be said to belong to Christ's flock. (John 10:26.) When the church views men and women, it asks first of all whether there are signs indicating that Christ has claimed them. If so, an appropriate address becomes this: "All things are yours, . . . you are Christ's; and Christ is God's." (1 Corinthians 3:21-23.) It is this sense of belongingness which has atrophied in our day, even among churchmen.

A similarly vast deterioration has taken place in the conception of membership. Each of us is a member of numerous organizations, and, though the organizations vary in significance and in power over us, the idea of membership tends to sink to a common low level of casual and tentative association. If one club doesn't suit, we can always shift to another. The same is true of church membership. My membership is wholly under my control, at least in a negative way. I can withdraw from an organization as soon as membership does not yield the results which I desire. My presence in the church is no exception. If I think of myself as a member in this sense, I think of all my fellows as being members in this limited sense as well. In a country where the mobility of population is high, most of us continue to think of our participation in the present congregation as temporary only. When we next move, we will move our membership with our household goods. The parish comes to consist only of those members who have not moved away.

But what did membership mean in the New Testament? There the term "member" did not refer to a person who had decided to join an organization, but to a constituent and necessary part of a living organism. A tongue is member of a body (James 3:5); so is an eye, a foot, a leg. (Matthew 5:29; 1 Corinthians 12:12-20.) The Christian is a member of *Christ's* body. The church is a body in no other sense than this. It is not a body of Christians, but the one body of Christ. So closely knit together is this body that the joy or pain of any one member is immediately shared by all the others. (1 Corinthians 12:25-26.) By being a member in this body, each is a member of all the other members. (Romans 12:5; Ephesians 4:25.) Each has, of course, a distinct function within the body, but membership in the body is quite incompatible with a jealously nurtured isolation or a cautiously conditioned commitment. It is the body and its needs which determine the life of its members and direct their work. A member could no more live apart from this body than a finger when cut from the hand. In fact, what it means to live is newly defined: "It is no longer I who live, but Christ who lives in me." (Galatians 2:20.) Many statements of this tenor provide the basis for Professor de Zwaan's description of church members: "All the gifts they possess and all the activity they display are a continuation of the work of Christ."

## In the World

This activity, of course, takes place in the world. There is, in fact, no other place for it to operate. And when the church is seen as the "sphere of action of the heavenly Christ," then the members of the church are seen also as constituting the frontier between the kingdom of Christ and the kingdom of Satan. We should not, therefore, in our exploration of horizons neglect this one. Here, for example, is a Corinthian who has become Christ's. If he belonged to Paul or Cephas or Apollos, the significance of his life would not be greatly changed. But he belongs to Christ, and this is not a partisan rallying cry, no sentimental exaggeration of a private conversion experience, no ambitious claim to esoteric knowledge, but simply a fact. The cross has demonstrated its power and wisdom by making him a slave of this severe yet merciful master. In himself, by being what he is, he is the representative of his nation, his city, his race, his economic class. In him as Christ's possession, all of these are embodied. By being what he is, he is the representative of Christ in every other circle of kinship, in every other sphere of duty. Through a person's baptism, Christ extends the range of his activity to include the far-flung and intricately woven web of relationships embodied in this person. Moreover, through the same baptism, this person, who embodies both himself and those in solidarity with him, brings them within the range of Christ's effective sovereignty. Now this event of baptism, as we have noted, has heavenly as well as earthly dimensions. Here the heavenly calling, the birth from above, becomes effective in the lives of men.

What has taken place in this event, both in heaven and on earth, is but the beginning of a process which points ahead to greater things. This process is far more than the life history of the individual who is baptized. His baptism is a divine promise of redemption for those from whom he is drawn and to whom he is now sent, a promise the fulfillment of which has now begun. Similarly, each drop of water in a lake represents all the water. Struck by a stone, this drop sends ripples farther than eye can reach. And when a boy tosses the stone, he knows that the nearest ripples will produce others. So, in the New Testament period, the conversion of one Gentile to Christ was taken as Christ's promise to save many Gentiles. And so long as one Jew "belonged to Christ" it was untrue to say that "God has rejected his people." (Romans 11:1.) The union of Jew and Gentile in one congregation was harbinger of an age in which there would be neither Jew nor Gentile. No family could be unaffected by the faith of father or mother. No city or province could be untouched by the gospel after one of its citizens had become a member of the Body of Christ.

So we detect another horizon of Christian community, no easier to chart than the others, yet no less far-reaching in its import. We find various signs of its presence in the thought of the early believer, but these signs remain elusive and even fanciful to later eyes. One such sign is the appearance of the figure "first fruit." To an agricultural people, the first grain to ripen symbolized the whole harvest. To the people of God, this first grain was God's promise that the whole harvest would immediately follow. They therefore sacrificed this first fruit to God as token of indebtedness and gratitude. Among the festivals of Israel few were more significant than the presentation of the first proceeds of the harvest, when the whole nation rejoiced over this new evidence of the Creator's bounty.

Under the new covenant two important meanings were added to this ancestral ritual. Celebration of harvest became eschatological in that God was now garnering his own grain into his kingdom. Therefore what had been an annual event became a symbol of a final event. Further, the initial proceeds of the harvest were no longer reckoned as grain or wine or oil but as the souls of men. Therefore the idea of the first fruits signified that this historical present in the life of the community intervened between the beginning of the harvest and its full reaping. Thus, when Paul wrote "Christ has been raised from the dead, the first fruits of those who have fallen asleep" (1 Corinthians 15:20), he was insisting that Christ's resurrection was the beginning of a general resurrection which would follow it as surely as the whole harvest follows the ripening of the earliest grain. Also, when in James we read "he brought us forth by the word of truth that we should be a kind of first fruits of his creatures" (1:18), we should interpret the existence of the church as the beginning of a creation-wide harvest, which will proceed until it is complete. If the Holy Spirit animates and empowers the work of this community, its presence here is guarantee of a work which ultimately will penetrate and redeem the whole universe. (Romans 8:23; 1 Thessalonians 2:13 margin; Revelation 14:4.)

This pattern of thought comes to a sharper focus when individual believers are called first fruits. So Epaenetus is singled out as the first fruit of Asia (Romans 16:5), and the household of Stephanas the first fruit of Achaia. (1 Corinthians 16:15.) This, of course, indicates that they had been the first individuals converted in their home provinces. But it means more than this. In being converted, they anticipate the conversion of the whole province. Their conversion constitutes the guarantee that the province, having through them accepted the gospel, now stands under the promise of God's salvation. For Epaenetus to become a member of this community was therefore a strategic event in the history of his province. His life became a beachhead of the kingdom in Asia. And what was true of Epaenetus was true in some degree of every member. For, in New Testament thinking, a person always represents not only himself but also that network of human bonds which constitutes him as a person.

There is, then, a vast range of symbolic meaning in belonging to God. The Son of man represented all men. His twelve apostles represented the twelve tribes of Israel. His seventy harvesters represented harvest to be reaped in all nations. (Luke 10:1.) The "tongues" present at Pentecost represented all languages, so confused since Babel. (Acts 2:8-11.) The church is intended to represent all nations, tribes, tongues, and peoples. The gospel must be preached to every form of human society, and every person who receives life through the gospel receives it for the sake of those who are kin to him. Accordingly, the community as it moves into the world has a boundary much more inclusive than its present roster of "members," for in each of them the existence of many others is involved.

## THE MINISTRY OF THE LAITY

We are witnessing in the twentieth century the recapture of this conception of Christian community. The recapture often appears in the form of a new doctrine of the laity. Along with other Christian words, this term has suffered drastic erosion in meaning, but its original force is slowly returning. The root of the original meaning is in the Greek phrase, the people (*laos*) of God. "The ministry of the laity" refers to the privilege and responsibility of this whole people to share in Christ's ministry to the world. Every member of the laity (*laos*) receives this privilege and this responsibility. In the church he represents his world. In the world he represents Christ's work. The most vigorous spokesmen of this truth may now be found within the World Council of Churches. Listen, for example, to this pronouncement of the Evanston Assembly:

In daily living and work the laity are not mere fragments of the church who are scattered about in the world and who come together again for worship, instruction and specifically Christian fellowship on Sundays. They are the church's representatives, no matter where they are. It is the laity who draw together work and worship; it is they who bridge the gulf between the church and the world, and it is they who manifest in word and action the Lordship of Christ over that world which claims so much of their time and energy and labour. This, and not some new order or organization, is the ministry of the laity. They are called to it because they belong to the church, although many do not yet know that they are thus called.[4]

All this indicates not so much a higher status for the layman in the church as a stronger sense of the church's presence in the layman. From the church's angle of viewing things, the life of the layman constitutes the boundaries of its own life. The significant moment is not when a person goes to church, but when the church goes into the world in the person of this representative. Now the layman's work becomes the church's work. Or more significantly, in Professor de Zwaan's phrase, the layman's activity becomes "a continuation of the work of Christ."

The ministry of the laity, thus interpreted, transforms the idea of what happens in the host of daily decisions which the layman makes. Just as the boundary between church and world cuts through his existence, so, too, it passes through each choice which he makes between conflicting ends and means. To revert to the image of the church as Christ's body, we may say that the whole body is at work in whatever any of its members is doing, and all members are present in whatever the body is doing. And Jesus Christ is "the One who is originating and coordinating this whole in order to realize the one final result." This, at least, is the perspective of the New Testament on matters of Christian behavior.

---

[4]W. A. Visser't Hooft, ed., *The Evanston Report*, New York: Harper & Brothers, 1954, p. 161. Used by permission.

Many different aspects of this perspective may become clear if the reader will turn to a single passage, Colossians 3:1—4:6. Here the apostle indicates the behavior which is consonant with being "called in the one body." (3:15.) The pattern of thought in the passage excludes many attitudes which in later days have become normal for many Christians. It is impossible, for example, in this passage to draw a sharp line to divide individual morality from group morality, because here every duty is so defined as to make the individual in his activity a representative of the "body's" activity. It is equally impossible to separate the area of inner motivations from outward deeds. The whole range of conduct, from the slightest subconscious desire to the most casual external act, must be redeemed from the "old nature" and come under the rule of the "new nature." (3:9-10.) Nor does the apostle allow the Christian to develop a double standard which encourages him to adopt one set of duties for services of worship and another set for the workaday world. The same "word of God" which produces songs of praise must produce deeds of gratitude "in the name of the Lord Jesus." (3: 16-17.) The walls which so easily can divide life into compartments are thus leveled: the wall between faith and conduct, between family and business (3:18—4:1), between sexual morality and greed for money (3:5), between racial prejudice and religious orthodoxy (3:11), between peace of mind and lowliness of status (3:12-15), between word and deed (3:8), between the treatment of friends and the treatment of enemies, between what a person *is* and what he *does*, between the ideal and the actual.

What power, we must therefore ask, is strong enough to destroy these compartments and restore to human life such integrity and wholeness? What strange force can bring into existence a community so closely knit together that impatience becomes as destructive as fornication (3:5, 12) and gracious speech to an outsider becomes as constructive as radical forgiveness to an insider (4:6; 3:13)? The answers to such questions, if complete, would make clear the uniqueness of this community; this uniqueness, in turn, would derive from the uniqueness of its relationship to Jesus Christ. We cannot give the complete answers, but we can indicate the directions in which such answers might be found.

This community, for example, is a body which is "nourished and knit together" by a "growth that is from God." (2:19.) Every member of this body has shared in the death and resurrection of its Head. (2:19; 3:3.) It participates now and always in the mysterious glory of God, the glory which enables heavenly power to appear in the form of earthly service. (3:1-4.) Its life is "hid with Christ in God." It is the realm where a new humanity is being created in "the image of its creator." (3:10.) In this realm "Christ is all, and in all." Therefore the Lord's deeds of forgiveness, kindness, meekness, and patience are being channeled through his body's acts of forgiveness. (3:12-13.) Over this body the peace of Christ rules (3:15); in it "the word of Christ" dwells richly. (3:16.) Everything done by the body and in the body is done in gratitude (vs. 17) and in fear (vs. 22) as a means of "serving the Lord Christ" (vs. 24). Or, to employ the idioms of our earlier chapters, we can say that the uniqueness of this community stems from its participation in the fullness of God's glory, in the warfare between God and Satan, in the city where God dwells, and in the time between the inauguration and the consummation of the coming kingdom.

The layman, to repeat, is a member of this community, and its representative in the world. In his words and deeds is to be discerned the frontier between the old age and the new. Whatever he does, however inconspicuous or trivial in the eyes of the world, signifies whether or not he is putting off "the old nature." (3:9.) When he chooses, the community is also choosing. When he chooses, he is choosing Christ or the devil, and is being chosen by Christ or the devil.

It was, of course, quite possible for the layman in the Colossian church to sunder himself from Christ and from the church; it was equally possible for the community to betray its Lord through the treason of its members. Moreover, this possibility was more than hypothetical. If there had been no actual danger, there would have been no need for the apostle to send his letter. If every church member, if every congregation, did *not* stand at the fateful point of choosing life or death, there would be *no* sense in speaking of the frontier as passing directly through the daily decisions of every member. Unless the church detects its own boundaries here, those decisions lose their significance. In the first as in the twentieth century, congregations were segregated, fearful, and enslaved to petty cant and cruel custom. But then as now, there was positive meaning in the fact that the Christian community is fully involved in the ambiguities and anarchies of what we call the social order, guilty of foolishness and futility, of weakness and hostility. The positive meaning lies here: these very contradictions do not allow us to forget that God has always chosen vessels of weakness and sin to manifest his power and righteousness. His kingdom is always given under conditions of a life authentically human; the eternal is always manifest in what is obviously temporal. As W. H. Auden has phrased it:

> For the new locus is never
> Hidden inside the old one
> Where Reason could rout it out,
> Nor guarded by dragons in distant
> Mountains where Imagination
> Could explore it; the place of birth
> Is too obvious and near to notice,
> Some dull dogpatch a stone's throw
> Outside the walls, reserved
> For the eyes of faith to find.[5]

In the midst of all its involvements in sin and death, where it seeks to redeem the time, the church cannot avoid asking again and again the question of its own identity.[6] "Who are we?"

---

[5] W. H. Auden *The Age of Anxiety*, New York: Random House, Inc., 1947, p. 135. Used by permission.

[6] In the remainder of this chapter I have used materials from my Dudleian Lecture, published in the Harvard Divinity School Bulletin in 1955 and used by permission.

"What is our relation to the Lord who is in the world?" "What is our relation to the world that is under the sovereignty of our Lord?" The church can have no adequate conception of its own identity without clarifying its position over against the world, and over against the God whom it worships. And for the clearest answer it will turn to the God who has disclosed himself in the world in Jesus Christ. To him the church, as long as it is the church, will turn for knowledge of its identity. The final standard of its own self-knowledge will not be an existing ecclesiastical practice, nor an idealized picture of historical possibilities, but the event of Jesus Christ in whom God unveils ultimate purpose and destiny. It is entirely legitimate, to be sure, to begin with the church as a familiar sociological entity and to move toward an empirical understanding of its historical functions. The church needs to see its face in mirrors which the world is only too eager to provide. But it is also necessary to begin with Christ, to observe how the Church is already comprehended and given in him, and then to move toward that self-knowledge of the church which is re-created whenever it proclaims the Lord's death until he comes. Quite obviously the church will utilize many finite images of itself, but for a living recovery of its unity and its freedom, it will again and again return to "the light of the knowledge of the glory of God in the face of Christ." (2 Corinthians 4:6.) And even in times when the church betrays its solidarity with Christ, it cannot escape the knowledge that it is known by One who will not release it from its call or its destiny.

## Destiny and Call

This Messiah has determined once and for all the call and destiny of the messianic community. Let us, then, draw together by way of a summary what characterizes this destiny and this call. Quite simply stated, the destiny is eternal life, or less simply but perhaps more accurately, eschatological life. The life of this community is eschatological, in the first place, because it embodies a movement from the beyond into the here, from God's world into our world. Whenever he speaks finally about himself, the God who is Omega and Alpha "speaks finally about the world of process." His purposive action moves from the coming age into the present, and links contemporary events firmly to their consummation.

Life in the Messiah is eschatological, secondly, because of the finality of the events through which it is mediated—the death and resurrection of Jesus. His death was his own death, the death of a man who dies once and not a second time. It was also the death of Adam and the death of everyman, since "he tasted death for all men." Such death is beyond doubt an eschatological category. So, too, is the Messiah's resurrection. His life-through-death is the life in which all shall be made alive. To him as first-born of the dead was given the power to beget the same life in those who "were dead through trespasses and sins." As John Robinson so well says: "Christians go to heaven, not at death, . . . but at baptism."[7] They then become not so much adherents of a religion as citizens of heaven. (Colossians 3:1-3.)

Life in the Messiah is eschatological, thirdly, because it discloses the present moment as the fullness of time. The demand for repentance transforms the ordinary day into the dawn of the Lord's day. Present isolation, present frustration, present despair, present idolatries of action—these are confronted with the word of the cross, with the promise of life through death. The God who was disclosed on Golgotha to believers and who will manifest himself to all in the Parousia is now pressing in on men and compelling them to a decision. Each present situation is laid bare as the scene of a critical choice. Wherever the crucified is acknowledged as the reigning Lord, there the thoughts of many hearts are revealed, secrets which otherwise would never have been known. The Messiah's cross is God's sword, slicing through pious self-deceptions and frantic self-justifications. The fire which he kindles is the refiner's fire by which

---

[7]From "The Christian Hope," in *Christian Faith and Communist Faith*, D. M. Mackinnon, ed. London: Macmillan & Co., Ltd., 1953, p. 213.

all men's works are tested. The warfare which he precipitates transforms human actions into fateful episodes in a final cosmic struggle between the Messiah and "the rulers of this darkness." The gospel turns the *now* into a point where the transient world meets the eternal kingdom, where the ego must crucify its pride and be reborn into life with the Messiah, into the brotherhood of the poor in spirit.

Finally, life within this brotherhood is eschatological because it "pre-enacts" the coming of the Messiah, when he will complete his work of subjecting every enemy. In Christ has taken place such an invasion of human affairs that nothing human and historical will in the end remain outside his kingdom. God has already given the Messiah dominion over death and life, over angels and principalities, over things present and things to come. In the end this dominion will be demonstrated to every creature. The gospel confronts men with the signs of this consummation and summons them to participate in the final conflict. Destiny always determines vocation. When the destiny is final, this vocation provides an ultimate beginning and end for the pilgrim journey. All this is so sweeping, so inclusive, so grandiose, that it is easy to forget what must not be forgotten—that the event through which the call came was the ministry of a humble Galilean carpenter who accomplished his messianic work on the ridiculed and obnoxious cross.

What, then, is the call which this Carpenter addresses to his church? And what sort of community does this call create? Perhaps the Greek word *koinonia* suggests an adequate answer. The usual translation is fellowship, but this rendering is altogether too subjective, too sentimental, too weak. C. H. Dodd prefers the idea of shareholding. "*Koinonoi* are persons who hold property in common" as joint owners. The solidarity is as objective and tangible as that. But *koinonia* goes much deeper than financial partnership, since Christians have been made partners with Christ and in him. They are joint heirs of a common life bestowed by him through the Spirit. This solidarity is so complete that what belongs to the whole community belongs to each member, and vice versa. "The life that is shared exists only as shared."[8] Sharing in this life changes the status of each partner and decisively redefines his existence.

It is because of this partnership in Christ that the church knows itself to be one. He shared fully in man's flesh and blood, in Adam's sinning and dying. His sharing with men established their solidarity with him. As Auden writes:

... Scorned on a scaffold, [he] ensconced in His life
The human household.[9]

Or as the Epistle to the Hebrews phrases it: "He who sanctifies and those who are sanctified have all one origin." (2:11.) He is not divided; neither is his body. The togetherness of the church in his death is, however, a complex rather than a simple fact. There is a oneness in the guilt for his death—Adam is Judas. There is a oneness in the enmity for which he prayed forgiveness, in the lostness of the world for which he died. The church also becomes one with him when it truly proclaims his death as God's power and wisdom. It becomes one with him in dying with him, the daily dying of repentance and the daily dying of a reconciling ministry. The church identifies itself both with his cry of dereliction and his assurance of victory. And in all these ways, participation in Christ's body means becoming members one of another, each counting the other better than himself.

This communion in the body of Christ conveys to the church solidarity with the living and returning Christ. In witnessing to the revelation of God in the cross and the resurrection, it witnesses to the coming epiphany of Jesus Christ with all who belong to him. By its very existence the church proclaims the Lord's death *until he comes.* It lives by the power expressed in the prayer, "thy kingdom come." But, as we have seen, this is no disjunctive futurism, because the Holy Spirit brings the coming kingdom into contact with the immediate struggle. In

[8]C. H. Dodd, *The Johannine Epistles,* London: Hodder & Stoughton, 1946, p. 6f.
[9]*Op. cit.,* p. 137.

praying for the kingdom, the church recognizes itself as a colony of heaven. It has been delivered from darkness into the dawn of a new day. It lives by the ingressive powers of the coming day, strengthened by the first fruits of the final harvest. The acts of repentance and love are acts by which the church opens the door to that love which will exercise the final power and the final justice. The fact that the church has a leasehold on the coming age does not encourage it to play with futures on the world's markets but to do its daily work in mills and fields. And it does this work in fear and trembling, for it knows of an impending judgment by the austere and impartial love of the Crucified. It knows that when his power is revealed, he will repudiate in a surprising way those who have deceived themselves by cheap grace and by cheap substitutes for obedience. As the spearhead of the advancing kingdom, the church knows that every fullness of time is marked by conflict and suffering before joy and glory can be revealed. *Koinonia* in the returning Lord is realized through sharing his warfare in the world. Knowledge of his crown comes through knowledge of his daily cross.

Partnership in this coming glory illuminates the human quandaries associated with futurity. The self-that-is-to-be and the church-that-is-to-be, these become real rather than hypothetical, assured rather than problematical. The destiny assured by God's prevenient grace becomes prior ground for present choices. Through this grace the believer and the church receive the confidence that all things (including things present and things to come) belong to them since they already belong to Christ. The ambiguous present is reperceived in the light of this dependable promise. Fears that death and nonbeing are man's final destiny are vanquished. Eternal life becomes "a silent knowing partner" of the self. The present and the future remain distinct tenses, but both are comprehended within the kingdom of Christ. The past with its fatalistic power of guilt and causation ceases to tyrannize the present. The future with its prospect of endless succession ceases to appall the weak or to bewitch the powerful. The present is restored to its rightful significance as the fullness of time, where men may realize the destiny to which God has called them. Knowledge of the end yields a hope purged of parochialism and a love freed from self-concern. Solidarity with the coming Christ thus produces solidarity in faith, hope, and love—gifts which manifest a basic reorientation toward time.

*Koinonia* with Christ, moreover, produces in the church a new solidarity with all other communities, the nations, races, tongues, and peoples which constitute the world. In every encounter with Christ the church meets a Lord "whose only concern is for others." His love is the point where the church sees God's omnipotence, omniscience, and omnipresence—the point where these divine attributes are redefined by the weakness, ignorance, and limitations of incarnation and death. His love is the measure both of God's distance and of his nearness. There were no limits to the love of him who was hung between two thieves. He established a solidarity with mankind at its lowest denominator: sin, flesh, futility, death. He was raised as the first fruits of God's harvest which will include all creation. The only line between his community and all others is drawn by a love which is so exclusive only because it is so inclusive. He welds into his community a genuine solidarity with all men, not last with the last, nor least with the least. He sets it in the world to bear the sin of the world and thus to serve as trustee of the world's reconciliation. Therefore, the sanctuary rightly stands not on the fringe of the city, but at its center, even though this means being destroyed in the holocaust of hydrogen bombs. "The church is her true self only when she exists for others."[10] Only thus can it maintain solidarity with him who has placed the stamp of the cross and the resurrection on all.

And finally, the church discovers that fellowship in Christ opens the door to a final freedom. The person who lives wholly for others is freed from self. Love brings the amazing gift of self-transcendence. The love by which the church is knit to-

[10]D. Bonhöffer.

gether unites it in an indestructible hope which frees it from the bondage to frustration. Its *koinonia* with Christ includes a gift of freedom, an eschatological freedom. In all other communities, the requirements of finite security create external restraints on personal freedom. Not so with the church. Here communal obligation and individual emancipation spring from the same person. The Lord who commands is the Lord who frees. The apostle who says, "I live, yet not I but Christ lives in me," must also say, "For freedom has Christ set you free." And this personal confession is the church's confession as well. Knowledge of itself as the possession of Christ conveys knowledge of a majestic liberty.

This freedom overcomes human bondage in many subtle ways. The act of repentance liberates the church from group egoism, from communal self-centeredness. The act of faith liberates it from anxieties of impending catastrophes and from unknown possibilities. The act of expectancy tears it loose from preoccupation with the past, from the stingy clutch of dead traditions. The act of trust gives it the courage to accept itself, to forget itself, to spend itself. The act of love frees it from compulsions to retaliate against earthly enemies. All of the acts by which it acknowledges God's gift elicit an open heart, an open future, an open world. It shares the frustrations of mankind, but it knows that no work which is done in the Lord is done in vain. It lives under the constant pressures of conventional moralities, of ecclesiastical ambitions, of cultural ideologies, of economic systems, of totalitarian nationalisms, but each re-enactment of the Advent and each pre-enactment of the Parousia restores the gift of a final freedom. *Koinonia* in that freedom makes the church the trustee of all those liberties of which the human spirit is rightful heir. Other human communities whittle down the freedoms of the individual when historical survival is threatened; the church celebrates a freedom given by God in the midst of catastrophe and death.

Catastrophe and death, of course, normally produce a tight constriction of freedom, because they enclose the human spirit within narrowing horizons and at last destroy the core of consciousness itself. But in the story of Jesus Christ, catastrophe and death produce the opposite results: new life for the self within expanding horizons. By celebrating his death and receiving his life, the church enters anew into its rightful inheritance of freedom because he gives to it the unlimited horizons of heaven on earth. Therefore, the church prays to him in the liturgy of St. Basil:

> According to the measure of our possibilities,
> O Christ, our God,
> The Sacrament of Thy will
> Has been fulfilled and completed,
> For we have had the memory of Thy death,
> We have seen the image of Thy resurrection,
> We have been filled with Thy eternal life,
> We have enjoyed this immortal food,
> Which grant us also in the age to come. . .